Revive us again

'For I will pour water on the thirsty land and streams on the dry ground'

Isaiah 44:3

Selwyn Hughes

Revised and updated by Mick Brooks

FURTHER STUDY: IAN SEWTER

© CWR 2014. Dated text previously published as *Every Day with Jesus: Heaven-sent Revival* (May/June 1989) by CWR. This edition revised and updated for 2014 by Mick Brooks.

CWR, Waverley Abbey House, Waverley Lane, Farnham, Surrey GU9 8EP, UK
Tel: 01252 784700 Email: mail@cwr.org.uk
Registered Charity No. 294387. Registered Limited Company No. 1990308.

All rights reserved. No part of this publication may be reproduced, stored in a retrieval system, or transmitted, in any form or by any means, electronic, mechanical, photocopying, recording or otherwise, without the prior permission of CWR.

Unless otherwise indicated, all Scripture references are from the Holy Bible: New International Version (NIV), Copyright © 1979, 1984 by Biblica (formerly International Bible Society). Used by permission of Hodder & Stoughton Publishers, an Hachette UK company. All rights reserved. 'NIV' is a registered trademark of Biblica (formerly International Bible Society). UK trademark number 1448790. Other versions used: Amplified: Scripture quotations taken from the Amplified® Bible, Copyright © 1954, 1958, 1962, 1964, 1965, 1987 by The Lockman Foundation. Used by permission. (www.Lockman.org) NKJV: *New King James Version*, © 1982, Thomas Nelson Inc. *Message*: Scripture taken from THE MESSAGE. Copyright © 1993, 1994, 1995, 1996, 2000, 2001, 2002. Used by permission of NavPress Publishing Group. Moffatt: *The Moffatt Translation of the Bible*, © 1987, Hodder & Stoughton.

Cover image: Getty/Flickr/ Benoit Paillé
Quiet Time image: photoalto.com
Printed in England by Linney Print

...very Day with Jesus is available in **large print** from CWR. It is also available on **audio and DAISY** ... the UK and Eire for the sole use of those with a visual impairment worse than N12, or who are ...gistered blind. For details please contact **Torch Trust for the Blind**, Tel: 01858 438260. ...rch Trust for the Blind, Torch House, Torch Way, Northampton Road, Market Harborough LE16 9HL.

A word of introduction ...

Revival. No other theme was closer to Selwyn's heart than this. As you may know, it was his passion from early childhood, having been brought up on stories of the 1904 Welsh Revival*. Some of his earliest family memories were of hearing about miners being overcome with conviction, falling to their knees to rise with completely transformed lives; of alcoholics miraculously transformed; of people going to public meetings to laugh and heckle but staying to pray and leaving transformed. It was always fascinating to hear Selwyn talk of these memories.

Revival later became a central focus of his talks and preaching. In fact, he talked about it so much that for a while he was known in his locality as the 'Revival Boy'. *Every Day with Jesus* was born and written as an aid to personal revival and in all the years I knew him he never lost that passion to see and experience true revival. Yet although he had been to many wonderful meetings, he never actually witnessed revival in what he believed to be the true sense of the word. His consistent concern was the use of the word 'revival' far too loosely - by calling almost anything a revival he believed that people become far too satisfied with less than the real thing.

He would have hoped that this issue, more than any other, would whet your appetite not only to embrace the fact of revival but to help us all into passionate believing prayer, providing a ramp across which revival is borne down from heaven.

Mick

Mick Brooks, Consulting Editor

*you can read more about these memories in *My Story*, Selwyn's autobiography, published by CWR.

Free small group resources to accompany this issue can be found at www.cwr.org.uk/extra. The *EDWJ* Facebook community is growing! To join the conversation visit www.facebook.com/edwjpage

Revival

FOR READING & MEDITATION – ISAIAH 44:1-8

'For I will pour water on the thirsty land, and streams on the dry ground' (v3)

We begin today a two-month exploration of what is without doubt one of the greatest themes of Scripture – heaven-sent revival. I say 'heaven-sent' because I believe revival is not something that springs up or out of the normal activities of the Christian church but something that comes down to us from above.

There are, of course, many different and conflicting views on this subject, so I want to begin by looking at a question I imagine no Christian will have any difficulty in facing: has God got something bigger in His heart for us than we are at present seeing? What is your response to that question, I wonder? Those who are privileged to be part of an active, vibrant church, or are actively involved in evangelism and social action projects, might respond differently from those who find themselves in a spiritually dry and dull place. But the truth is (in my opinion) that no matter how spiritually alert and alive the community in which you work and worship, God is able to do even more. Our God has reserves of power which we, the Church of this generation, have not fully experienced. I'm not sure anyone could disagree with that!

Whilst we are not unappreciative of the fact that God is clearly sending showers of blessing upon His Church, we must not forget either that the God who sends the showers can also send the floods. In fact, revival is just that – God flooding a locality or a community of His people, stirring up the complacent, and producing the conviction and conversion of a great number of people. It has happened at various times in various places throughout history, and as sure as night follows day it will happen again.

FURTHER STUDY

Isa. 11:1-9; John 14:6-14

1. What is God's full intention?

2. How can we do greater things than Jesus?

O Father, whilst I see the need for a greater outpouring of Your Spirit upon Your Church, my initial prayer is not corporate but personal: Lord, send a revival and let it begin in me. In Jesus' name I ask it. Amen.

Defining revival

FOR READING & MEDITATION – ACTS 3:11–26

'... that times of refreshing may come from the Lord' (v19)

Today we ask: what is revival? Unfortunately the word has no sharp edges and so everyone who uses the word has to define what they mean by it. Many years ago, when I first visited the United States, I was asked by a minister if I would preach at the revival his church would be having in a few weeks time. I remember being somewhat surprised at his faith and presumption in predicting the exact date of a revival, until I was informed by a friend of mine that in that part of America, and at that time (as I say, many years ago) the term 'revival' simply referred to a series of special meetings.

In this series of devotional studies I am using the word in its classic sense to denote an unexpected, awesome and overwhelming flood of God's power upon a community of His people. D.M. Panton describes spiritual revival as 'an inrush of divine life into a body threatening to become a corpse'. Christmas Evans, an old Welsh preacher whom God used to stir the nation of Wales on several occasions, had this to say about the subject: 'Revival is God bending down to the dying embers of a fire just about to go out and breathing into it until it bursts into flame.' Quite simply, revival means 'to wake up and live'.

I personally know of no better definition of revival than that given by J. Edwin Orr who, in his book *The Second Evangelical Awakening in Britain*, wrote: 'Revival takes place when we experience "times of refreshing from the presence of the Lord".' Whichever way we look at it, revival is life at its best, life in all its fullness, life abundant, life overflowing with the grace and power of God.

FURTHER STUDY

Psa. 72:6–19; Isa. 35:1–7

1. What are the characteristics of God's reign?
2. How can a barren desert be fruitful?

O Father, this matter of revival has the feel of the real and the eternal upon it. Awaken within me a deep desire for a 'time of refreshing from the presence of the Lord' – personal as well as corporate. In Jesus' name. Amen.

What revival is not

FOR READING & MEDITATION – HABBAKUK 3:1-19

'... O LORD, revive your work in the midst of the years!' (v2 NKJV)

As it is vitally important to be quite sure what we are talking about when we use the word 'revival', we spend another day exploring its meaning. G. Campbell Morgan, the great preacher of a bygone generation, defined it like this: 'Revival is the reanimation of the life of the believer, not the unregenerate as they are "dead in sin". There can only be revival where there is life to revive.'

Revival always begins, not with the conversion of the godless, but with the reanimation of the people of God. That is why it is probably a mistake to see evidences of spiritual revival in meetings and events where hundreds or thousands of people are converted. Great evangelistic plans and advances are currently being made here in Britain and around the world, but this must not be seen as revival. Evangelism is the expression of the Church; revival is an experience in the Church. Evangelism is the work man does for God; revival is the work God does for man.

Revival is much greater, also, than the restoration of backslidden Christians. There are times in church life, such as during conferences, large events, summer festivals and other activities, when large numbers of Christians make a new and deeper commitment to Jesus Christ. This, of course, is wonderful and is something for which we are deeply thankful – but it is not revival. Again, some of the large healing services we hear about, where hundreds of people are healed and wondrous miracles take place, are not revival. We can see people converted, renewed, restored, healed, and yet fall short of revival. Revival includes all these things yet surpasses them all.

FURTHER STUDY

Ezek. 37:1-14; Psa. 85:4-6

1. How may God work with man to produce revival?

2. What happens when people are revived?

Gracious and loving Father, the more I meditate on this subject of revival, the more I long to experience it. You have visited Your people in times past in great and awesome power. Do it again, dear Lord. Do it again. Amen.

SUN
4 MAY

Why we need revival

FOR READING & MEDITATION – 2 CORINTHIANS 1:3-14

'But this happened that we might not rely on ourselves but on God, who raises the dead.' (v9)

We have seen that revival is 'a time of refreshing from the presence of the Lord'. Today we examine the question: why do we keep on needing such experiences? Why can't we hold on to revival when it happens? Why, for example, did the Christians in Wales during the revival at the beginning of this century – in 1904 – allow the fire that swept the Principality to die out?

We can find the answer to these questions by understanding the history of God's people as found in the Scriptures and in the early Church. In the Old Testament, we see that there were times when God's people were at the dizzy heights of spiritual blessing and power, only to plunge later into spiritual apathy and despair. Even after the great outpouring of the Spirit at Pentecost the Church, one generation later, lapsed into lethargy and indifference so that in Revelation 2 and 3 we see our Lord having words with the seven churches of Asia with the challenge to repent and return to their first love. History tells us that by the beginning of the second century AD the Church seemed to have dwindled in influence and power and it was not until hundreds of years later that it revived and began once again to make an impact upon the world.

FURTHER STUDY

Isa. 53:6; Dan. 4:24-37

1. What is our natural tendency?

2. What did the king come to realise?

Note carefully what I am now about to say – the major reason for all spiritual lapse is rooted in the *desire for independence*. Initially, when we enter into a new relationship with God, we are conscious of a great sense of dependency upon Him, but unfortunately after a while something rises up within us and clamours for more independence. And it is this, more than any other single thing, that causes us to let go of what God gives us.

O Father, help me to look within my own heart and evaluate to what extent the desire for independence rules my life. Show me even more clearly, dear Lord, that if I do not crown You Lord of all, I do not crown You Lord at all. Amen.

CWR Ministry Events

PLEASE PRAY FOR THE TEAM

ATE	EVENT	PLACE	PRESENTER(S)
-8 May	Bible Discovery: Revelation	Pilgrim Hall	Philip Greenslade
May	Bible in a Day	Waverley Abbey House	Andy Peck
-16 May	May Country Break	PH	
May	A Bridge Too Far – Insight into the Forgiveness Journey	PH	Mary Higginson
May	Managing Conflict Creatively	WAH	Chris Ledger
2 May	Christ Empowered Living	WAH	Mick & Lynette Brooks
June	Spiritual Formation for Leaders	WAH	Viv Thomas
June	Jesus' Best Sermon? (Part one) Free summer evening for homegroups	WAH	Andy Peck
June	Revolutionise Your Devotional Life	WAH	Andy Peck
8 June	Women's Weekend: Knowing True Joy	PH	Paula Buchel & team
13 June	Introduction to Biblical Care and Counselling	WAH	Angie Coombes & team
-15 June	Marriage on Track	WAH	Lynn & Andrew Penson
June	Women's Summer Day: Hearing is Believing	PH	Gail Dixon
June	Jesus' Best Sermon? (Part two) Free summer evening for homegroups	WAH	Andy Peck
-22 June	Bible Discovery Weekend: Strength Made Perfect in Weakness	WAH	Philip Greenslade
June	Counselling Enquirers Event	PH	
June	Below the Surface – Understanding Eating Disorders	WAH	Helena Wilkinson
June	Preaching from the Gospels	WAH	Andy Peck
June	Ready Answer: Building Confidence in Your Faith	WAH	Andy Peck

ease also pray for students and tutors on our ongoing **BA in Counselling** programme Waverley and Pilgrim Hall and our **Certificate and Diploma of Christian Counselling** d **MA in Integrative Psychotherapy** held at London School of Theology.

r further details and a full list of CWR's courses, phone +44 (0)1252 784719 visit the CWR website at **www.cwr.org.uk** Pilgrim Hall: **www.pilgrimhall.com**

The swings of history

FOR READING & MEDITATION – JEREMIAH 2:4-13

'They have forsaken me, the spring of living water, and have dug ... broken cisterns that cannot hold water' (v13)

We continue meditating on the thought we touched upon yesterday, that one of the major reasons why we experience dryness and spiritual dehydration (and need to be revived) is our natural and stubborn commitment to independence. Historians talk about the swings of history, and as far as the people of God are concerned, no swing is more evident than the swing from dependency to independency.

The reason I have chosen the chapter that is before us today is because it highlights, perhaps better than any other passage in the Bible, this matter of independence. This is something we explore in great detail in our counselling courses and it is a constant theme in all aspects of the ministry at CWR. Note the charge which God brings against the children of Israel: 'But my people have exchanged their Glory for worthless idols' (v11). This bears down on the fact that Israel was not as loyal to God as the pagans were to their own gods – a fact so astonishing to God that He calls on the heavens to bear witness to it (v12). Next, He indicts them for failing to drink from the fountain of living water which He provides for His people and for turning instead to cisterns that can hold no water (v13).

Can you see what had happened to Israel? They had started off in absolute dependence on God – worshipping only Him and drinking from His fresh wells – but after a while they had felt within them the urge to take control of their spiritual lives and manage them as they thought fit. And whenever God's people do this, no matter how positive and seemingly active their spiritual life may be, they are desperately in need of revival.

FURTHER STUDY

Deut. 8:1-18; 1 Cor. 11:23-26

1. What might Israel forget?
2. What should we remember?

God, how it saddens You that we Your Church, like Israel of old, start off depending on You, the invisible God, but then rely on things that are more visible and more tangible. Forgive us, Father. Forgive me. In Jesus' name. Amen.

The stepping stone

FOR READING & MEDITATION – HOSEA 14

'Take words with you and return to the LORD. Say to him: "Forgive all our sins"' (v2)

Nothing is more destructive to see within the people of God than the desire for self-control and self-dependency. This is not because of any selfishness in God that requires Him to be the boss, but because He knows that when we try to run our lives on our own terms we often fall short of His plans and purposes for us. We must face the fact that as human beings we were created dependent and that God and God alone is independent. He can exist without us but we cannot exist without Him.

The periods of revival in the Old Testament came at the high peaks of corporate worship in the life of Israel, when the people acknowledged the fact that they could not successfully run their lives on their own terms but were successful and effective only to the degree that they were dependent upon God. In the chapter before us today we see how God called His people back to dependency upon Him by encouraging them to repent: 'Take words with you, and return to the LORD.' This means (so I believe), 'Have a clear idea of what you are repenting of.'

The stepping stone from independency to dependency is always through the door of repentance. There is simply no other way that it can be done. That is why in all revivals the issue of repentance and dependency becomes paramount. In revival God underlines in a vivid and dramatic way the truth that the path to a continuous and continued relationship with Him is through continuous repentance. The key to all change is in a returning to God, for every effort to change must invoke at its core a shift in direction – away from dependence on one's own resources to dependence on the living God.

FURTHER STUDY

Gen. 3:1-8;
Rom. 1:18-32

1. How does man try to be independent?
2. What is the result of this independence?

Father, I see that if I stumble here, over this matter of dependency and independency, I stumble all down the line. Help me not to deny this issue but to face it and repent of it. I do so now. In Jesus' name. Amen.

'The shop is always open'

FOR READING & MEDITATION – REVELATION 3:14–22

'So, because you are lukewarm – neither hot nor cold – I am about to spit you out of my mouth.' (v16)

Having briefly considered some of the elements of a spiritual revival, we now consider some of the arguments of those who believe that revival is irrelevant in today's Church. Sadly, some say the Church is a religious institution similar to the institutions of law and medicine. And just as these institutions have the resources and provisions to meet the needs of those who wish to draw upon them, so also has the Church. The exponents of this view say that the Church possesses everything she needs to live an effective life here on earth – sacraments, hallowed forms and traditions of worship, fellowship, and so on. If someone is spiritually sick, so they say, all they have to do is make their way to the Church and they will find there the medicine they need for their soul.

Emyr Roberts and Geraint Davies in their booklet *Revival and Its Fruit* take issue with this view and say of it: 'In this sense the Church exists independently of the congregation; if nobody calls, the shop is always open.' There can be little doubt that one's view of revival depends on one's view of the Church. Those who see the Church as an institution rather than a community of people brought into being and maintained by the influences of the Holy Spirit and the Word will see the whole issue of revival as unnecessary and irrelevant.

But what is the Church? It is not a building but a body – a body empowered and made alive by the Holy Spirit. And the secret of her survival in this world is in continually opening herself to the Spirit who gave her life. She was not only born of the Spirit but survives and thrives by the Spirit. No Spirit – no life.

FURTHER STUDY

Acts 4:1–17; 1 Cor. 12:1–13

1. How did religious institutions view the Sprit's work?

2. What do we have in common?

Father, I see that unless the red blood of the Spirit's energy and power flows through the veins of the Church she becomes weak and faint and anaemic. Give us, oh give us, a greater flow of Your life and power. Start it in me today. Amen.

Too cramped for comfort

FOR READING & MEDITATION – 2 CORINTHIANS 3:1-18

'... where the Spirit of the Lord is, there is freedom.' (v17)

We continue looking at the Church as a religious or divine institution. Those who see the Church in this light believe (as we said) that the Church exists independently of the congregation. It is easy to see how anyone holding this view of the Church will have little interest in the subject of spiritual revival. They will be interested not in passion and intensity, but in order and stability. They will not merely regard revival as irrelevant, but as downright messy, even injurious. It interferes with the smooth functioning of the services and breaks into the well-established forms and ceremonies.

The revivals of the past have often been opposed by those who have seen the Church as an institution, for the work of the Holy Spirit cannot be brought under human control. A revival can be untidy and even undignified, with people crying out in the midst of a sermon, or striking up a song at a seemingly inappropriate time. Whenever institutional Christianity has been faced with a movement of the Spirit that did not fit into its preconceived ideas of how the Church should function, it has immediately set its face against it.

During the Middle Ages, when the Church as an institution was at its strongest, the Spirit tried to break in and reveal Himself to His people, but as history clearly records, the leaders resisted these winds from the Spirit. As a result, those who felt the Spirit's touch abandoned the institutionalised Church and met together to enjoy Spirit-directed activity and worship. I do not think God despises institutional Christianity; it's just that sometimes it gets too cramped for comfort, and He has to move out.

FURTHER STUDY

Acts 15:1-11;
1 Cor. 14:26-40

1. How did some believers react to the Spirit's work?

2. Should church meetings be a 'free for all'?

Father, help me to have a right view of the Church for I see that the way I look at this, and every, issue affects all my attitudes. Help me to take Your way, even though it cuts across my nature. In Jesus' name I pray. Amen.

FRI
9 MAY

'The pulse beat of all we do'

FOR READING & MEDITATION – JUDGES 16:1-22

'"I'll go out as before ..." But he did not know that the LORD had left him.' (v20)

We continue exploring the view that the Church is a religious or divine institution. My dictionary defines the word 'institution' as 'an establishment for the cure of souls'. In a sense then, the Church is an institution, but it is not *essentially* an institution. Essentially it is a body, an organism, through which life and energy must continually flow if it is to experience vitality and health. And the life that must flow through the Church is the life that comes from the Spirit. He and He alone gives life. I say 'He' for the Holy Spirit is more than an influence. He is a person who guides, counsels, cleanses, empowers, directs, and most of all, abides with us. An impersonal influence, an 'it', doesn't do that.

Have you ever wondered why it was that at Pentecost the Holy Spirit did not fall in the Temple but in the Upper Room? I have thought long and hard about this for many years and for what it is worth my conclusion is this – if the Holy Spirit had been given in the Temple, then His coming would be associated with a sacred place, sacred services and sacred occasions. The Holy Spirit came in the most common place – a home. He is not given for special 'spiritual' occasions, but for all occasions – for all life.

The Holy Spirit is not a spiritual luxury to be imported into the unusual but a spiritual necessity at work in the usual. He is to be the pulse beat of all we do – the Life in our living. And when He is absent or not permitted to have full control, the Church, like Samson in our text today, might shake itself and make a great fuss but will succeed in accomplishing nothing.

FURTHER STUDY

1 Sam. 16:14; Acts 16:6-10, 18:9-11

1. How was Saul's experience similar to Samson's?

2. How was the Spirit the pulse beat of Paul's ministry?

Gracious and loving Father, I am so grateful that I do not have to wander from sacred place to sacred place in search of Your Spirit. You come down to me wherever I am and turn all my seculars into sacreds. Amen.

A scandal to Christianity

FOR READING & MEDITATION – 1 THESSALONIANS 5:12-22

'Do not put out the Spirit's fire.' (v19)

Today we look at another argument advanced by those who think revival is an unnecessary and irrelevant issue. It is sometimes expressed in this way: 'A religious revival is nothing more than a manifestation of crowd hysteria.' For example, one critic of the Welsh revivals says: 'Welsh people are easily moved. Their fiery nature and love of singing makes them easy prey to the emotional and the melodramatic.' There is some truth in those words, of course, but it is not all the truth. It takes more than emotionalism to explain the fact that during the 1904 revival in Wales crime dropped to such a degree that many of the courts were closed and some of the pubs went out of business.

Peter Price, a strong critic of the Welsh revival, saw in it nothing more than tumult, noise, play acting and imitation. Those who believe that religious worship should not contain any show of emotion are offended by the commotion and untidiness of spiritual revival. Thomas Morgan, a nonconformist minister writing about the Methodists of his day said: 'It appears to all true and serious Christians that they (the Methodists) are stark mad and given to a spirit of delusion, to the great disgrace and scandal of Christianity.'

But those who ridicule revival for what they call its extremes of emotion would do well to reflect on those occasions in Scripture when people appear to be beside themselves in the presence of God. Whilst we must be cautious about excesses of emotion we must make equally sure that we do not quench the Spirit by intellectualism and unwillingness to accept the supernaturalism that is everywhere portrayed in the Scriptures.

FURTHER STUDY

2 Sam. 6:16-23; Acts 7:51-60

1. How did Michal respond to David's enthusiasm?

2. What was Stephen's view of religious leaders?

God, help me not to be the one who quenches Your Spirit. Whatever it may be that causes me to draw back from asking and believing for greater and bigger things, then root it out of me today. In Jesus' name I ask it. Amen.

The poorer language

FOR READING & MEDITATION – 1 CORINTHIANS 2:6–16

'The man without the Spirit does not accept the things that come from the Spirit ... they are spiritually discerned.' (v14)

We spend another day examining the objection we looked at yesterday, that revival is merely a manifestation of crowd hysteria. One eyewitness of a revival meeting in Anfield Road Chapel, Liverpool in 1905 said, 'Crowds were pressing against the chapel doors trying to push their way in, elderly ladies were climbing over the railings to get to the door and falling on the others, and some were being thrown inside by the police like sacks of flour.'

Critics who read such reports as this ask: 'Is there any difference between the religious madness seen in times of spiritual revival and the frenzies and ecstasies associated with the celebrities and personalities of the present day?' On the surface there appears to be little difference; the immediate sensations and the conscious nervous impressions may be very similar. But, as C.S. Lewis pointed out in *Screwtape Proposes a Toast*, the tongues phenomenon on the Day of Pentecost might also have appeared to an onlooker to be nothing but an expression of nervous excitement or hysteria.

When we try to express the spiritual through the natural it is like translating from a richer to a poorer language. In the poorer language you have to use the same word to express more than one meaning, and it is the same when you try to express the richer world of the spirit through the poorer medium of the physical frame. We have only laughter to express both ribald revelry and godly joy; we have only tears to express the most selfish, worldly grief and the most godly sorrow. Therefore we must not be unduly surprised that spiritual rejoicings are mistaken for rejoicings of a very different kind.

FURTHER STUDY

Neh. 8:9–12; Isa. 55:8–13

1. From where do we gain spiritual strength?
2. Why may people not understand God's ways?

Gracious Father, give me the ability to think through and see deep into the reason for things. Quicken my spirit so that I can recognise the truth in everything and thus be more open to everything. In Jesus' name I pray. Amen.

Help us to provide pastors and church leaders in the poorest nations of the world with the inspiration and teaching they so urgently need ...

The turbulence across the developing world is obscuring a thrilling change – a great crying-out for the truth of Jesus. The rising number of Christian converts is great, and so the pressure on new pastors is increasing, creating an urgent need for quality Christian literature to send to pastors, leaders, colleges and libraries in several of the world's poorest nations.

This is where CWR comes in: our plan is to arm each pastor entering the ministry over the next two years with a hardback copy of our 1,600-page *Cover to Cover Complete* NIV Chronological Bible. Pastors will be able to read the whole Bible in a year, in sections with inspiring commentaries by Selwyn Hughes, all clarified with maps, timeline charts and illustrations. It is a pledge we can bring to life only with your support.

CWR will cover the costs of publishing the Bibles and getting copies to some of the most remote rural locations abroad, assisted by the charity Sovereign World. We estimate those costs will amount to just £12 per Bible. Your gift now of one or more copies will be much appreciated.

Please fill in the 'Gift to CWR' section on the order form at the back of this publication, completing the Gift Aid declaration if appropriate.

An excitement that goes nowhere

FOR READING & MEDITATION – PSALM 145:1-13

'One generation will commend your works to another' (v4)

I remind you that the question we are considering at the moment is this: is revival a manifestation of crowd hysteria? We have seen that although on the surface there may appear to be little difference between the scenes reported at meetings where revival has broken out and the frenzy and excitement observed in many of today's pop and rock concerts, underneath there are great differences.

Let me deal with just one difference – the matter of the final outcome. A crowd coming together for a music festival experiences a high degree of emotion and excitement, but what does it result in? A family member of mine who is not a Christian and who attended a recent festival said to me: 'It was tremendously exciting being there but the trouble is, the excitement doesn't go anywhere.' Compare this with the excitement and energy that was evident on the Day of Pentecost. It was excitement and energy that went somewhere.

Charles Foster Kent says, 'On the Day of Pentecost this pent up feeling broke out into an irresistible wave of spiritual enthusiasm that marked the beginning of the worldwide Christian missionary movement.' I have a little problem with his phrase: 'a pent up feeling breaking forth into an irresistible wave of spiritual enthusiasm' for it was not an enthusiasm worked up by circumstances but an infusion of the Holy Spirit. However, he is right when he says it 'marked the beginning of the worldwide Christian missionary movement'. When God moves in revival the energy, authority and excitement goes somewhere – it influences and affects not just the present but also the coming generations.

FURTHER STUDY

Isa. 51:1-11; Luke 2:8-20

1. How can our enthusiasm and joy last for generations?

2. Describe the impact of Jesus' birth.

O God, whatever excitement fills my soul as a result of my contact with You, let it go somewhere. Grant that it might not stay in my feelings but be translated into light and energy by which I might walk. In Jesus' name I ask it. Amen.

Don't get tipped off balance

FOR READING & MEDITATION – 2 TIMOTHY 3:16–4:5

'... that the man of God may be thoroughly equipped for every good work.' (v17)

We look now at another argument advanced by those who see the issue of revival as unnecessary and irrelevant. It goes like this: 'Encouraging people to believe for a revival serves only to make them spiritually discontent and too heavenly minded to be any earthly good. They become so preoccupied with praying in a revival (which happens only infrequently) that they fail to get on with the task at hand.' I have some sympathy with this argument as I too have been concerned for years over those Christians who talk a lot about a coming revival but in doing so avoid the day-to-day responsibilities of Christian living.

Many years ago, when I was a minister in Wales, I knew a church whose leaders firmly believed that they should cancel all their usual activities and hold a prayer meeting every night of the week until God sent revival to their community. Once committed to this seemingly spiritual but rather misguided idea, they simply had to keep going and they continued holding prayer meetings every evening for over a year, after which the congregation were so tired and bewildered they were obliged to call a halt. The church has never recovered to this day.

Think of all the opportunities which the people in this church missed in evangelism and outreach because they had an unbalanced view of the subject of revival. They thought they were being guided, but they failed to see that their commitment to pray every evening until revival came was more an obsessive demand than a deep spiritual desire. When the issue of revival becomes an obsession, it can eventually tip us off our spiritual balance.

FURTHER STUDY

Neh. 4:1-9; Acts 12:1-17

1. How did Nehemiah combine prayer and action?

2. How did Peter interrupt his own prayer meeting?

Father, help me differentiate between the demands that arise from my own nature and the spiritual desires which arise out of Your inner prompting. For I see that one is an open road; the other is a cul-de-sac. In Jesus' name I pray. Amen.

WED
14 MAY

Is revival an obsession?

FOR READING & MEDITATION – EPHESIANS 3:14-21

'Now to him who is able to do immeasurably more ... according to his power that is at work within us' (v20)

We looked yesterday at a church whose commitment to pray every evening until revival came was more an obsessive demand than a deep spiritual desire. This raises the question: what is an obsession? An obsession is a repetitive or persistent thought or idea which crowds into the mind and helps to relieve one's basic anxiety. At worst, it is really a defence mechanism which enables the personality to avoid anxiety by focusing not on the anxious feelings but on the continuing or recurring thought instead.

Some years ago I talked with a young psychologist who told me that he had made a study of the temperaments of people who continually wrote and talked about spiritual revival and had found an interesting pattern – all of them tended to be obsessive. I offered to take the psychological test he had devised and it showed that although I was determined and single-minded, I was also able to change – something an obsessive person cannot do. When I saw he was convinced that I was a fairly well-adjusted person, I talked to him about my own preoccupation with revival. And he said I was the exception that proved the rule!

I have no doubt that by reason of their temperament some Christians can become obsessed about anything – including revival. But I also know that around the world I have come across an army of well-adjusted Christians who are discovering within their hearts at this time in history a deepening desire to see God work in great and mighty power. Some may see it as an obsession; I see it as a possession – the thoughts of God taking hold of the thoughts of man.

FURTHER STUDY

Num. 21:6-9; 2 Kings 18:1-4; Isa 62:1-7

1. How had the Israelites formed an obsession of God's provision?

2. Why should we give God no rest?

Father, whilst I do not want to be the victim of an obsession, I most certainly want to be the recipient of divine possession. I give You the freedom to occupy my whole being and to think and feel in me day by day. Amen.

How to wait for revival

FOR READING & MEDITATION – LUKE 19:11-27

'Put this money to work ... until I come back.' (v13)

We continue looking at the argument that encouraging people to pray for revival serves only to make them spiritually discontented, so much so that they fail to get on with the tasks at hand. I recognise that this can happen, but it need not happen if clear Biblical teaching is given by those whose responsibility it is to expound the Scriptures.

Permit a personal testimony here: I have been talking and writing about revival ever since I came into the ministry thirty-nine years ago, and although it has been a major preoccupation of my life (not an obsession!), I have always encouraged people not only to pray for revival but also to be sure that other responsibilities, like evangelism, fellowship, and Bible study, are not neglected.

In the text before us today our Lord tells us, 'Occupy till I come' (v13 AV). I take this to mean that He wants us to get on with the task of representing Him to the world no matter what may be the conditions around us. Those who say, 'Let's give up working and just wait and pray for God to send revival,' fail to understand the Scriptures. Evan Roberts prayed several hours a day for thirteen years for God to send revival to Wales, but he still went about his daily tasks and made sure that nothing was left undone. The same can be said of others who have figured greatly in past revivals.

A good example to follow in relation to this is one that was given to me early in my ministry and one which I keep constantly before me. Like most mottoes, it has some flaws but it makes good spiritual sense nevertheless: work as if all depended on you, and pray as if all depended on God.

FURTHER STUDY

1 Cor. 15:50-58; 2 Tim. 4:1-5

1. What did Paul advise in the light of Christ's return?

2. What work was Timothy to do?

Gracious and loving heavenly Father, make me a responsible and balanced person, I pray. Help me to keep up my prayer life without neglecting the other responsibilities that You have given me. I want to occupy until You come. Amen.

Taking a qualitative look

FOR READING & MEDITATION – PSALM 146

'The LORD reigns for ever, your God, O Zion, for all generations. Praise the LORD.' (v10)

We look now at yet another issue put forward by those who see revival as unnecessary and irrelevant. Put in its simplest form it goes like this: the fruits of revival do not last.

The fact must be faced that not all who make a profession of faith during a time of revival continue to follow Christ after the fire has subsided. It would be foolish to deny that some of the fruits of revival do not last. Critics claim that out of the many converts won to Christ in the United States during the 1859 revival, only a small proportion could be found in the Church ten years later. The same criticism has been made against the revivals which have taken place in other countries.

How do we answer this argument? The fruits of revival, I submit, ought to be looked at qualitatively and not just quantitatively. Take, for example, my native Wales. I believe that if it had not been for the revival that stirred the Principality in 1904, the Christian presence there today would be almost non-existent. During revival sometimes only one member of a family is converted, but that one person often influences a whole family.

I regard myself as a product of revival. My grandfather was converted to Christ in the Welsh revival of 1904. He influenced my mother who, together with my father, greatly influenced me to give my life to Jesus Christ. How many families who are now in the Christian Church might be outside had it not been for the fact that some distant relative or ancestor was won to Christ during a time of revival? The duration of a revival may be comparatively short and brief but its results spill over into succeeding generations.

FURTHER STUDY

2 Tim. 1:1–2:2

1. What was the source of Timothy's faith?

2. What was he to do with his faith?

Father, I am beginning to understand that there is more to revival that I first thought. Thank You for helping me to see that the influences of revival never stop – they pass from one generation to the other. I am grateful. Amen.

Fruit that lasts

FOR READING & MEDITATION – PSALM 78:1–8

'... we will tell the next generation the praiseworthy deeds of the LORD' (v4)

We continue looking at the argument that the fruit of revival does not last. While it is true that some of the fruit does not last, it is not true that none of the fruit lasts. When revival is measured qualitatively and not just quantitatively we see that its benefits and fruit spill over into the next generations.

Some of the greatest preachers the world has seen have been men who were converted during the time of revival. It is said that at the funeral of Daniel Rowland of Llangeitho in October 1790 (the man who was greatly used by God in revival in Wales in the eighteenth century) over one hundred ministers were present, many of them having been won to Christ during the days of that revival. Sidney Evans, a man who has written a great deal about the subject of revival said, 'The revivals of past history have often safeguarded the Christian ministry for a whole generation.' And when you consider the influence ministers have in inspiring young men to enter the ministry you can see that a revival safeguards the ministry not just for one generation but for many generations.

Then take the staggering number of converts who have been swept into the Kingdom of God during times of revival. The revival in America in 1859 claimed a million converts and a further million in the British Isles, one hundred and ten thousand of those in Wales alone. These numbers are staggering and even allowing for the fact that not all may have been genuinely converted, it is obvious to a fair-minded and reasonable person that the spiritual impact of these large numbers of converts cannot help but have an influence on future generations.

FURTHER STUDY

Deut. 4:5-14; Psa. 71:14-19

1. How might we benefit from teaching our children?

2. What was David's commitment?

Father, help me understand that the river of revival never really stops. It may disappear for a while but it continues to flow on – underground. Thank You, dear Father. Amen.

Steps to helping others

'Carry each other's burdens, and in this way you will fulfil the law of Christ.' **Galatians 6:2**

God puts compassion for the hurting into the hearts of people for this reason: He can completely transform lives and He wants to work through us. At the heart of CWR's ministry is the desire to equip people with the biblical foundations and counselling skills needed to serve God in this way and effectively help others.

Perhaps you or someone you know would like to help people in your community or church. Our team of lecturers and counselling practitioners offer professional training within a unique and proven Christian framework. Whether you would like to gain basic counselling skills or study to post-graduate level, you can take the steps opposite as far as you wish.

'I have learnt so much about God, about myself, and about helping others to explore who they are and who they can be in Christ.'

STEP 1 Introduction to Biblical Care and Counselling (5-day course)

STEP 2 Waverley Certificate of Christian Counselling (ACC Level 3) - (BA Counselling year 1)

STEP 3 DipHE Counselling - (BA years 2 and 3);
OR BA Counselling (Hons) - (BA years 2 to 4);
OR for graduates: MA Counselling (2 years)

STEP 4 For trained and experienced counsellors:
MA Relational Counselling and Psychotherapy (2 years)

We don't want anything to hold back those wanting to train in counselling. Our training is flexible and progressive; if you have already completed any of the steps elsewhere you may be eligible for direct entry into a later step. Most of the courses are part time and the time you take to complete a qualification can be extended to fit around the demands of work and home.

Courses are held at our two centres
in Surrey and East Sussex
For more information or to apply, contact the Admissions Office:
T: +44(0)1252 784719
E: training@cwr.org.uk
W: **www.cwr.org.uk**

Why things are not worse

FOR READING & MEDITATION – PSALM 102:18–28

'Let this be written for a future generation, that a people not yet created may praise the LORD.' (v18)

Although the Church community, the representation of Jesus on earth, is sadly sometimes in conflict with itself, things might well be worse were it not for the fact that the influences of previous revivals still reverberate in our midst. The same, I think, can be said of the secular world. Here in the UK our society faces many struggles and difficulties, morally and spiritually, but I believe things would be much worse were it not for the continuing influence of the great revivals of history.

This must not be taken to mean that the prayer life and godly living of present-day Christians make no contribution to our world, for clearly they do. We the people of God in this present generation provide 'the salt and light' that make it more difficult for evil to prosper. That said, however, the impact of past revivals can still be felt at work in our generation – even in our Houses of Parliament where the words of Psalm 127:1 'Unless the LORD builds the house, its builders labour in vain' encircles the floor of the central lobby.

Many years ago I was part of a small group who visited the Houses of Parliament to present a specially produced Bible to the Prime Minister of the day – Harold Wilson. Whilst there, we had the opportunity to talk to several Christian MPs who, amongst other things, informed us that the origins of many of the laws and statutes by which our land is run can be traced back to the times when our nation was in the midst of spiritual awakenings. I know it is a sobering thought with which to begin the day, but we might well ponder what kind of society we would find ourselves in at this moment were it not for the great spiritual awakenings of the past.

FURTHER STUDY

Psa. 147:7–20; Prov. 29:18

1. Why was Israel blessed?

2. What happens when there are no godly laws to follow?

Gracious and loving heavenly Father, how can I sufficiently thank You for the way You have revived Your people at intervals throughout history? I sense the past at work right here in the present – and I am grateful. Amen.

Mixed experiences

FOR READING & MEDITATION – 2 PETER 3:10-18

'... grow in the grace and knowledge of our Lord and Saviour Jesus Christ' (v18)

Today we examine one more reason why some people regard the issue of revival as unnecessary and irrelevant – the fact that emotions kindled in revival are not unmixed spiritual experiences. Critics point out that revival brings to the fore not only the spiritual side of man's nature but the physical and more worldly side too.

Here again we must listen to the truth contained in this criticism before attempting to answer it. It is true that in revival the spiritual is often mixed with the worldly. Williams put it like this: 'When our soul came to taste the feasts of heaven, the flesh also insisted on having its share, and all the passions of nature aroused by grace were rioting tumultuously.' And this was at the high point of the Methodist revival when none can deny that the Holy Spirit was amazingly at work. Revival does not abolish in one fell swoop human nature or the defects of our nature.

In the years immediately following the great outpouring of the Spirit at Pentecost there were clear evidences of flawed human nature at work. Paul's letters are full of exhortations to resist this and to subdue the works of the flesh. The great revivalist Jonathan Edwards said that if the people in the Corinthian Church had been left to themselves they would have torn themselves to pieces – yet clearly the Spirit was at work in their midst – we know this because the apostle greets them as 'the Church of God ... called to be saints'.

We will never fully understand revival until we understand its primary purpose. And what is that? It is not to bring saints to perfection in a day, but to wake up the drowsy.

FURTHER STUDY

1 Cor. 1:10-17, 5:1-6:8

1. What problems were in the Corinthian church?

2. Why is it better to be wronged than right?

Father, thank You for reminding me that revival, like conversion, does not produce instant saints. Help me see that although character may come out of a crisis, it is more often the result of a process. In Christ's name I ask it. Amen.

TUES
20 MAY

The Delectable Mountains

FOR READING & MEDITATION – 1 PETER 1:3–12

'... you ... are filled with an inexpressible and glorious joy' (v8)

We continue with the point we ended with yesterday, that the primary purpose of revival is not to bring saints to perfection but to wake up the drowsy. 'The cultivation of Christian virtues, and the building of sound and sane Christian character,' says Emyr Roberts, 'is the work, under the blessing of God, of the pastor and the teacher.' Sublime and joyous feelings, however, have their place, and nowhere are these felt more keenly than in the time of revival.

Listen to what one person says about his experience of revival: 'Thursday night the 22 December 1904 will be inscribed in letters of fire on my heart for ever! Don't ask me to describe what I felt that night – I can never do it! All I can say is that I felt the Holy Spirit like a torrent of light causing my whole nature to shake. I saw Jesus Christ – and my nature melted at His feet. I have done nothing since Thursday night but to sing to myself that hymn: 'O, the love of Jesus'. And today I feel I belong to everybody. Oh how the love of Christ expands a man's heart.'

We readily agree with the critics of revival that such an elevated emotional state cannot last, and it would be misguided to expect that one could live continuously in the energy of such exaltation. This does not mean, however, that there is no point or purpose to such feelings. One supporter of revival says of such experiences: 'They are like a walk on the Delectable Mountains from whose heights we are given a glimpse of Mount Zion. We have to walk generally by faith and not by sight but on our pilgrimage it is no small thing to catch a glimpse of the heavenly city and to know a foretaste of its felicity and bliss.'

FURTHER STUDY

Psa. 48:1-14; Gal. 5:22-23

1. Where do we find the joy of the whole earth?

2. How are joy and the Spirit linked?

Father, day by day my appetite for revival is being whetted. I see that only an invasion from heaven can produce the impact to turn both the Church and the world in Your direction. Grant that it may come soon. In Jesus' name I pray. Amen.

No need for a fire extinguisher

WED
21 MAY

FOR READING & MEDITATION – 2 TIMOTHY 4:9-18

'... Demas, because he loved this world, has deserted me' (v10)

The fact that Christians can come down from the heights experienced during times of great spiritual awakening and lose their first love and joy, is not a valid argument against revival. As we have seen, we have only to examine the New Testament to find that following the outpouring of the Spirit at Pentecost there were some who seemed to lose their joy and slip back into old patterns of independent behaviour. Yet none can deny the reality and genuineness of the presence of God that surged in their midst.

Critics of revival also draw our attention to the fact that revival can sometimes induce great spiritual pride – especially in the young. Revival history contains many accounts of young men being carried away by pride after a high peak in their spiritual experience. William Williams says of one: 'He was a raw youth whom no one would entrust to shepherd his sheep and is riding high in a boldness of spirit much superior to old ministers who have borne the burden and heat of the day.' But then, were there not such people in the Church that emerged after the Day of Pentecost? In one place Paul warns against appointing a novice in the faith to office in the Church, 'lest being puffed up with pride he fall into the same condemnation as the devil' (1 Tim. 3:6 NKJV). Sadly, it is a failing that at one level must be expected, guarded against and understood.

Revival is potentially full of pitfalls – let us not argue against that – but all the dangers can be met and handled through the principles that are set forth in the Word of God. When a coal falls out of the fire no reasonable person rushes for a fire extinguisher. They simply pick up the tongs and return the coal to the grate.

FURTHER STUDY

Prov. 26:20;
1 Pet. 5:1-11

1. How might revival be extinguished?

2. What is the solution to pride?

Father, help us as Your Church not to draw back from praying for revival because of the obvious dangers that accompany it. Show us that when we keep close to You we are equipped to handle anything that comes. Thank You, dear Father. Amen.

Getting ready for revival

FOR READING & MEDITATION – HEBREWS 10:19–25

'... encourage one another – and all the more as you see the Day approaching.' (v25)

We spend a final day reflecting on the argument that the emotions kindled in revival are counter-productive to an effective Christian life. The answer, as we have seen, is that this can be so – but it need not be. When Biblical truth and application is available from wise men and women to channel the high energy and emotion seen in times of revival into productive purposes, then the sky's the limit.

Many who witnessed the 1904 Welsh revival say it could have continued longer and made an even greater spiritual impact if there had been more teachers and teaching resources to lead the people into the deeper things of God. When I first learned this (just after becoming a Christian in my mid-teens), I immediately committed my life to doing everything I could to ensure that future revivals would not suffer for lack of teaching resources.

In 1965 I founded the Crusade for World Revival (now called CWR) with the primary objective of encouraging people to pray for both personal and corporate revival and deepen their understanding of the Word of God. Other goals and objectives have been added to these over the years, but the primary goal is still that of helping God's people prepare for revival. I like to think that day by day as you peruse the pages of *Every Day with Jesus*, read the set scriptures and digest the notes, you are not only building up your own spiritual resources but preparing yourself for a deeper and more effective ministry to others – now and in the future. Who knows but that in addition to your present and daily ministry for Christ you may have a part in establishing someone who has come to know Him in a time of revival?

FURTHER STUDY

Ezra 7:6-10; Neh. 8:1-18

1. How had Ezra prepared himself for revival?

2. How did he prepare the people for revival?

O Father, how wonderful it would be to witness a revival – and have a part in it. But whether I will or not, help me to take the knowledge I gain from You day by day – and pass it on. In Jesus' name I ask it. Amen.

What good is light without life?

FOR READING & MEDITATION – ISAIAH 59:9–21

'When the enemy comes in like a flood, the Spirit of the LORD will lift up a standard against him.' (v19 NKJV)

From what we have been saying over the past few days, it is quite clear that when revival comes it contains not only unlimited blessing but very real pitfalls. It is also clear that *despite the dangers* the very survival of the Church depends on the timely and reviving work of the Holy Spirit.

There are some who think the Church is now so strong she does not need revival. A magazine article I saw the other day said: 'The Christian Church is stronger now than she has ever been throughout her entire history. Numerically, there are more people in the Church today than at any other period of her existence. She is well-represented in almost every nation under the sun and if she would become aware of her strength and size *and draw upon it* she could dominate the world and have it sitting at her feet.'

The words and phrases sound good but what are the facts? The Church may be numerically strong and well-represented in different parts of the world but since when has her strength been in her numbers? The source of her strength and power is in the Holy Spirit. Without His presence in the Church, energising and reviving, there may be plenty of light, but little life. And it is *life* – the life of the Spirit – which the Church so easily loses.

Generally speaking, the Church has been good at protecting its theological position, but not so good at preserving life. That is why at certain times and in certain generations God mercifully breaks in upon His people to revive and refresh them by the Spirit. In every century the Christian Church has stood in need of a new invasion of that life. But perhaps never so much as now.

FURTHER STUDY

2 Cor. 3:1–6; Gal. 3:1–5

1. Contrast the letter of the law and the Spirit.

2. Why did Paul criticise the Church?

Father, help me see that no matter what else Your Church has, if it does not have life – the life of the Spirit – then it is no more than a religious club. Breathe upon us for we want not only to be living, but lively. In Jesus' name. Amen.

'Revival praying'

FOR READING & MEDITATION – ISAIAH 64:1–12

'Oh, that you would rend the heavens and come down' (v1)

Having explored the debate surrounding the issue of revival, we next need to consider the place which prayer plays in the bringing about of revival. Without doing any injustice to the sovereignty of God, the next question we must face is this: what kind of praying is it that seems to precipitate a mighty and extraordinary move of God?

A phrase which crops up time and time again in revival literature is the phrase 'revival praying'. This is a term used to describe the inspired praying which historians have noticed takes place in the months or years preparatory to the outbreak of revival. Over the next few days I want to examine with you some of the characteristics of this inspired prayer sometimes referred to as 'revival praying' and I hope by so doing to deepen our understanding and awareness of this mysterious and intriguing but deeply important subject.

Firstly, 'revival praying' is *passionate* praying. People pray with an intensity and enthusiasm. It is not that they look with disregard upon formal prayers but, almost as if they cannot help it, their prayers catch alight and are uttered with what appears to onlookers to be uncharacteristic energy and enthusiasm. They become not only enthusiastic about their prayers but eager in the pursuit of them. They spend time in the presence of God, wherever they can, and with whomsoever they can. Prayer becomes less of a duty and more of a delight. I am sure you have occasionally touched something like this in your own prayer times but prior to a revival it is not just something that happens periodically but something that happens regularly, not just in a few scattered places, but generally.

FURTHER STUDY

1 Sam. 1:1–28

1. How did Hannah pray?

2. How was she perceived by religious authority?

Father, I long to experience more passion in my prayer life. I throw open every aspect of my life to You today. Move into the whole of my life, but especially my prayer life, and set my prayers on fire. In Jesus' name I pray. Amen.

The story of Jeremiah Lanphier

FOR READING & MEDITATION – PSALM 69:1–15

'... zeal for your house consumes me' (v9)

We continue looking at passionate praying or inspired prayer, which we said yesterday is one of the characteristics of revival praying. An example of what I mean by this type of praying comes out of the story of the great revival which hit New York in the middle of the nineteenth century.

On 1 July 1857 a man by the name of Jeremiah Lanphier, described as 'a quiet and zealous businessman', took up an appointment as city minister in the Dutch Reformed Church in New York. He decided to hold a noon-day prayer meeting and distributed a few handbills inviting others to join him during the lunch hour every Wednesday. At the first meeting six people were present. The second week there were twenty and the third week over forty. It was then decided to hold the prayer meeting every day. Within months, 10,000 people were gathering in the city every day to pray. Thus began in New York the spiritual awakening which eventually spread through America and in 1859 crossed the seas to the British Isles. Inspired praying – the kind that precedes revival – usually begins with one person in an area and then spreads to others. I know of no revival where this has not happened.

How can we explain it, this presence of God that inspires God's people prior to revival? What is it that makes them want to be present at as many prayer meetings as they can get to and pour out their hearts in earnest supplication to God? There is only one convincing explanation – it is a supernatural phenomenon. The heart of revival is beyond psychological or sociological explanation. If in prayer we have great intention, then God gives greater attention.

FURTHER STUDY

1 Kings 19:1–18; John 2:13–17

1. What motivated Elijah?

2. What motivated Jesus?

Father, I have already asked You to give me more passion in prayer; now I must take it. I reach out with empty hands to receive the fullness of Your Spirit. From now on my prayer life shall be Spirit-taught and Spirit-wrought. Amen.

MON
26 MAY

'Great prayer warriors'

FOR READING & MEDITATION – GENESIS 32:22–31

'... I will not let you go unless you bless me.' (v26)

We look now at the second characteristic of revival praying or inspired prayer – tenacity and persistence. Read the record of revivals and you will find that this quality is also present. In the days prior to revival people not only pray zealously but they pray persistently. For over a period of thirteen years Evan Roberts prayed for revival to come to Wales. 'There was never a day,' he says, 'when I didn't fling myself before God and cry out for Him to send the Holy Spirit to my native land.' Dafydd Owen also prayed every day for over ten years for a great outpouring to come to the Principality. And it was said of David Morgan 'that for ten years before 1858 a petition for the outpouring of the Holy Spirit was never absent from his prayers'.

FURTHER STUDY

Matt. 7:7–12; Luke 18:1–8

1. What is the difference between asking, seeking and knocking?

2. What did Jesus explain about prayer?

It is important to recognise that often this persistence was not something that was normal for these great prayer warriors of bygone days but was given to them by the Holy Spirit. It was said of Evan Roberts that when he was a boy 'he hardly ever saw anything through and would give up a task most easily'.

Listen to what Jonathan Edwards, another great revivalist, has to say about the importance of persistence and perseverance: 'It is very apparent from the Word of God that the Lord is wont often to try the faith and patience of His people, when crying to Him for some great and important mercy, by withholding the mercy sought for a season; and not only so but at first to cause an increase of dark appearances. And yet He, without fail, at last succeeds those who continue instant in prayer with all perseverance and will not let Him go except He blesses.'

Father, search my heart today and see if there is any hidden thing in me that holds me back from persistent and persevering prayer. Bring it to the light so that I can deal with it. I ask this in Jesus' name. Amen.

A revival is on the way

FOR READING & MEDITATION – EPHESIANS 6:10–20

'And pray in the Spirit on all occasions with all kind of prayers and requests' (v18)

We continue looking at the quality of tenacity or persistence as a component of revival praying. Prior to a revival this characteristic is often seen even in those who were not naturally persistent or tenacious people and this is fairly clear evidence (so I believe) that something supernatural is at work.

When the news of the American 1857 revival reached the shores of Great Britain many churches (especially those in Northern Ireland and Wales) became gripped with a desire to see the same thing happen here. William Jenkins, the minister of a church in one of the Welsh valleys, said in 1858: 'Ever since the news of the outpouring of the Spirit upon the American churches reached our country I longed and prayed that the Lord would, in His infinite mercy, visit poor Wales. I immediately brought the subject before the church and earnestly exhorted them to 'seek the Lord'. I related every fact and incident I could glean ... in order to produce in the minds of my people the desire for a similar visitation. Some of our members prayed *and continued to pray* as I have never heard them pray before. A new burden seemed to press upon their hearts. They became persistent almost to the point of being obsessed. Even before revival came there were no less than eighty-five added to the church in about six months' (italics mine).

Examples of persistent and tenacious praying gripping the people of God prior to a revival can be multiplied. They have made such an indelible mark in history that those who observe, watch and wait for their occurrence are able to say with confidence, 'A revival is on the way.'

FURTHER STUDY

Rom. 8:26-27; 1 Tim. 2:1-8

1. How does the Spirit help us pray?

2. What was Paul's desire?

Father, I cannot help but echo the words of Your disciples: 'Lord, teach us to pray.' In this area I confess I am entirely weak, but help me see that in You I am able for anything. So I shed my weakness and take Your completeness. Amen.

God – sleeping on the job?

FOR READING & MEDITATION – PSALM 44:13-26

'Awake, O Lord! Why do you sleep?' (v23)

A third characteristic of God-inspired revival prayer is boldness or directness. Here again I have been struck, as I have read and researched this subject, by the daring and direct language used by God's people when seeking Him on this issue of revival.

We can see something of this in the verses that are before us today. The psalmist appears to be accusing God of sleeping on the job. Listen to the graphic language used in *The Message* translation of this passage: 'Get up, GOD! Are you going to sleep all day? Wake up! Don't you care what happens to us? Why do you bury your face in the pillow? Why pretend things are just fine with us? And here we are – flat on our faces in the dirt, held down with a boot on our necks.' This is direct and daring language by the psalmist but it would seem it is the kind of attitude and language that prevails with God.

Notice that I say *attitude* as well as language. You and I can come before God and use similar language but if it is not accompanied by the kind of holy desperation that the psalmist felt, then it is only manipulative and demanding, false and hollow – even impertinent. Such was the spiritual decline around him that it looked to the psalmist as if God was asleep and needed arousing. His deep concern over the declining conditions with which he was surrounded made his language appropriate and permissible. When we feel as strongly about the moral and spiritual bankruptcy that surround us as the psalmist felt in his day, then we can speak as strongly as he did. But be warned: we dare not copy the words unless we are also prepared to copy the psalmist's deep spiritual concern.

FURTHER STUDY

Gen. 18:16-33; Acts 4:23-31

1. How was Abraham bold and direct?

2. How did the early Church pray?

God, my concern at this moment is not so much whether You are awake but whether I am awake – awake to the urgent needs that lie all around me. Wake me up, dear Lord, and help me pray with boldness and concern. In Jesus' name I ask it. Amen.

Prayer God delights to answer

FOR READING & MEDITATION – PSALM 59:1-8

'O LORD God Almighty, the God of Israel, rouse yourself to punish all the nations' (v5)

We spend another day looking at this quality of boldness and directness which seems to be a characteristic of all revival praying. There is a fine line, of course, between impertinence and concern. To some it may appear that the psalmist has crossed the line and entered the realm of impertinence. Telling God to rouse Himself hardly seems to be a reverent or respectful way of approaching the Almighty. But, as we said yesterday, it is the attitude of ultimate understanding of God and who He is that makes it permissible.

I have often heard people in prayer meetings try to copy the strong language of the psalmist and other Old Testament characters but I have never felt, except on a few occasions, that they had the psalmist's same burning concern. And lacking that concern, their prayers came across as empty and hollow. One biographer tells of listening to the great Christmas Evans praying before the outbreak of revival in a certain part of North Wales. This is what he said: 'Wake up, O Lord, and shake Yourself. Can't you see what is happening to Your Church? It's shameful that You allow things to go on like this. Do anything – do something– and do it soon.'

The biographer went on to say: 'Those who heard him caught their breath and wondered why God did not strike him dead for his impertinence. But what they did not know was that Christmas Evans had earned the right to talk to God in this way.' He was not just using language – he was expressing through that language the deep concern of his heart. And when those two things combine – passion and daring – you have the ingredients of the kind of prayer that God delights to answer.

FURTHER STUDY

Matt. 15:21-28; John 2:1-11

1. What qualities did the woman in need show?

2. How did Mary's request affect Jesus?

Father, once again I have to confess that my feet stumble on the path of prayer. There is so much to learn, so help me over the hard places. This is life and I must learn it. In Jesus' name I pray. Amen.

'Pleading the promises'

FOR READING & MEDITATION – PSALM 119:25-32

'Revive me according to your word.' (v25 NKJV)

We look now at a fourth characteristic of revival praying, which I am calling *persuasiveness*. As the word is sometimes used to convey the idea of being coercive or pushy, however, permit me to give it a more narrow and precise definition. One of my dictionaries defines it in this way: 'The art of being able to marshal one's arguments in a convincing way so as to leave the other person or persons little or no option.' This exactly sums up what I have in mind when using the word in relation to revival or inspired and extraordinary praying.

FURTHER STUDY

2 Kings 19:9-37

1. What did Hezekiah place before God?

2. What was the result?

Here again, when examining the great prayers that precede revival I have been struck by the way in which the men and women concerned build and develop their arguments on the basis of what God has said in His Word. You might have already noticed in the psalm before us today that the psalmist founds his plea for divine quickening on the fact that God has promised it in the Scriptures: 'Revive me *according to your word*.' Some people call this 'pleading the promises' – the art of taking a clear promise which the Lord has made, reminding Him of it and insisting that He be held to it.

Charles Spurgeon, when teaching on prayer, used to say: 'Every promise of Scripture is a writing of God which may be placed before Him in reasonable request, "Do as Thou hast said." The Creator will not cheat the creature who depends upon His truth; and far more the heavenly Father will not break His own word to His own child.' Our forefathers discovered that prayers which plead the clear promises of a covenant-keeping God are guaranteed success – it is time we discovered it too.

Father, the concept that You are a covenant-keeping God fires my faith and energises my spirit as I know nothing else can. You are showing me a way of prayer that is breathtakingly powerful. Help me to know how to use it. Amen.

What is a promise?

FOR READING & MEDITATION – 2 SAMUEL 7:18–29

'And now, LORD God, keep for ever the promise you have made ... Do as you promised.' (v25)

We ended yesterday with the thought 'prayers that plead promises are guaranteed success'. This raises this question: what is a promise? A promise has been described as, 'A written declaration that binds the person who makes it to do or forbear to do a specified act.' When used of God, it is His pledge or undertaking to do or refrain from doing a certain thing. Such promises form the basis of the prayer of faith and it is through prayer that they are turned into facts and factors of one's Christian experience.

The validity and dependability of any promise rests on the character and resources of the one who makes it, just as the validity of a bank cheque depends on the honour and bank balance of the one who signs it. It is the holy character and faithfulness of God that makes all His promises credible. 'Not one word has failed of all the good promises,' said King Solomon (1 Kings 8:56). Those who have studied the great prayers of the Old Testament will have noticed the way in which those prayer warriors continually reminded God of the promises He had made. We see it, for example, in the passage before us today: 'Do as you promised.'

It is not presumptuous to take God at His word, providing we are sure that the promise He has made applies to our particular situation.

Note that last statement, for it is extremely important. The requests in verses 25 and 26 of today's passage are built on the promises in the previous verses. In revival praying men and women stretch their desires to the width of God's promises and hold God to the pledge He has made that times of refreshing shall come from the presence of the Lord.

FURTHER STUDY

Heb 6:10–20; 2 Pet. 1:3–11

1. How do we receive God's promises?

2. What promises has God given us?

O Father, I see that this throws open infinite possibilities to me. But I see also the danger of holding You to a promise that is not relevant or applicable. Give me the wisdom to know the difference. In Jesus' name. Amen.

'Are my hands clean?'

FOR READING & MEDITATION – JEREMIAH 14:17–22

'O LORD, we acknowledge our wickedness and the guilt of our fathers' (v20)

A fifth characteristic which can often be observed in God-inspired revival praying is a new and fresh commitment to walk in holiness. Even the most casual reader of the Old Testament cannot help but notice that whenever the leaders of the people approached God with the plea of revival they usually began by acknowledging their own sin and the sins of the people. Jeremiah does it in the passage before us today: 'We acknowledge, O LORD, our wickedness and the iniquity of our fathers ... Remember, do not break Your covenant with us' (vv 20–21, NKJV).

FURTHER STUDY

Rev. 2:1-7; 2 Cor. 7:8-13

1. What steps should the Ephesians take to revival?

2. What are the results of godly sorrow?

Every well written and carefully researched report of revival I have read contains the record of people coming before God prior to the revival and openly confessing their sins. The Hebrides Revival which took place in 1949 is a classic illustration of this. A group of people knelt to pray in a barn about twelve miles north of Stornoway and kneeling in the straw one of them, a young deacon, opened up his Bible and read from Psalm 24: 'Who shall ascend into the hill of the LORD? or who shall stand in his holy place? He that hath clean hands, and a pure heart' (vv3–4, AV).

After reading the passage twice the young man said, 'Brethren, it is just so much humbug to be waiting thus night after night if we are not right with God. I must ask myself: is my heart pure? Are my hands clean?'

And at that moment something happened. Let Duncan Campbell, the man who wrote up the account of the Hebrides Revival, finish the story: 'God swept into the barn, whereupon the group moved out of the realm of the common and the natural into the sphere of the supernatural. And that is revival.'

Father, I see that the depths of prayer hold challenges for me which only a full and determined commitment can meet. I have come a long way with You, Lord, now help me go further. My hands are outstretched to You – pull me through. Amen.

A sure sign of revival

FOR READING & MEDITATION – PSALM 32

'Then I acknowledged my sin to you and did not cover up my iniquity.' (v5)

We are seeing that prior to revival the prayers of God's people are characterised by contrition and a desire to break with all known sin. The closest I have ever come to witnessing what I am describing here was during a visit to Korea in 1958. As you know, the nation of Korea has been experiencing a great religious revival since the beginning of the 1960s but in the year that I was there, although the people were greatly expectant, the Church could not be described as being in revival.

One morning I participated in a 4 am prayer meeting – an event I shall remember for the rest of my life. As I entered the prayer venue – a large school assembly hall – I was conscious that I was about to witness something unusual. The place was crowded and there was a tense reverent attention on every face. There was no singing and at a given signal people knelt for prayer. At first there was silence but soon the people began to pray aloud, one after the other, until within seconds their voices became a crescendo which then stopped as suddenly as it had begun. A man's voice rose in high-pitched tones and my interpreter told me that he was confessing his sins and the sins of the nation. No words of mine can adequately describe the intensity that was in his voice, the agony of his sobs and the penitence that seemed to grip him. Within minutes the same spirit of penitence spread through every heart in the audience – my own included.

I came away from Korea sensing that I had witnessed the first stages of a spiritual revival. When later I heard that revival had broken out I was not surprised. The signs had told me so.

FURTHER STUDY

Jer. 3:1-18; 1 John 1:8-10

1. Why might God withhold showers of blessing?

2. What is God's promise if we repent?

O Father, help me never to forget that Your name is called Jesus because You save Your people from their sins. I know I am saved but now I ask – save me to the uttermost. In Christ's name I pray. Amen.

Labour pains

FOR READING & MEDITATION – NEHEMIAH 1

'I sat down and wept. For some days I mourned and fasted and prayed before the God of heaven.' (v4)

We look now at the final characteristic of revival praying – spiritual God-inspired heartache. People who intercede powerfully for revival are often heartbroken but determined. My old pastor, David Thomas, used to say to me when I was a young Christian: 'If ever there is to be another revival in our nation, then it will be borne in on the shoulders of desperate men.'

One of the best illustrations I know in the Old Testament of spiritual desperation is Nehemiah. When he heard of the pitiable condition of his fellow countrymen he reacted deeply. He was told: 'The survivors there in the province who escaped exile are in great trouble and shame; the wall of Jerusalem is broken down, and its gates are destroyed by fire' (v3 RSV). Look at the reaction of Nehemiah when he received this news: 'When I heard these words I sat down and wept, and mourned for days; and I continued fasting and praying before the God of heaven' (v4).

Commentators point out that we do not read of any other Jewish exiles reacting in this way. Nehemiah could easily have turned his attention to other things, but his heart was so sensitive to God that he became spiritually desperate. Arthur Wallis, commenting on Nehemiah's reaction to the news that the walls of Jerusalem were reduced to rubble, says 'His feelings ... were the labour pains out of which a new movement of God was born.'

Nehemiah was so desperate to see God work that he not only prayed but fasted as well. People have to be pretty desperate to go without food! How desperate are you in connection with the need for revival? Desperate enough to do something about it?

FURTHER STUDY

Ezra 9:13–10:6; Acts 13:1–3

1. What motivated Ezra to fast?

2. What happened when the early disciples fasted?

Father, You are working in my life. I know You do it to develop me. Help me, I pray, to know something more of what it means to be spiritually desperate. In Jesus' name I ask it. Amen.

Desperate men

FOR READING & MEDITATION – PSALM 143

'I spread out my hands to you; my soul thirsts for you like a parched land.' (v6)

We continue looking at the characteristic of spiritual desperation which, we have been saying, usually makes its presence known in all revival praying. I believe it was Karl Barth who once said: 'We do not read our Bibles aright until we read them like desperate men.' He meant, I think, that until we become spiritually desperate ourselves we will not be able to recognise the desperation that flowed in the hearts of men and women who are portrayed in the Scriptures.

I wonder, as you read the psalm that is before us today, did you feel the desperation that is present in the heart of the psalmist? Commenting on this psalm, C.S. Lewis observes that the first eleven verses were obviously written by a desperate man as the chosen words bring tears to the eyes of the reader. Of course, the psalmist here is praying for personal revival and not national revival, but the principle to get hold of is this – desperate praying brings powerful and positive results.

Permit me once again to ask you a personal question: have you ever felt desperate enough about the moral and spiritual conditions around you to spend a few days praying and fasting? Some people's response to the idea of fasting is: 'Well things are not desperate enough to demand that!' There's an old saying that goes: 'Desperate situations demand desperate measures.' I don't know how you view the world situation, but it seems to me that things are in a desperate state. And they will only change as the desperation in the world is met and countered by a holy desperation in the hearts of the men and women who constitute the Christian Church.

FURTHER STUDY

2 Chron. 20:1-30

1. How did God's desperate people respond to invasion?

2. What was the result?

O Father, use what I have read today to drive me to Your feet in a spirit of holy desperation. Help me to bring those things to your throne, so that revival would start with me. In Jesus' name. Amen.

Are you available?

FOR READING & MEDITATION – GALATIANS 1:11–24

'I did not consult any man ... but I went immediately into Arabia and later returned to Damascus' (v16–17)

Over the past days we have been looking at some of the marks of God-inspired revival praying – the unusual characteristics that seem to be present in the intercessions of those who feel deeply burdened for revival. We have highlighted six of these characteristics (though of course there are many more) – first, passion; second, persistence; third, boldness; fourth, persuasiveness; fifth, contrition and sixth, desperation.

We now ask ourselves: how is it that these characteristics reveal themselves? Is it something that God puts into people's hearts or is it something that arises out of the conditions that are around? Probably it is a combination of both. Oswald Chambers has the key to it, I think, when he says: 'Whenever God plans to send revival blessing He first lays a burden for it on the hearts of those who make themselves available to Him.' Note the phrase: *'those who make themselves available to Him'.* Oswald Chambers tells the story of how an aged saint came to his pastor one night and said: 'We are about to have a revival.' The pastor asked him why he thought this, whereupon the old man replied: 'I went into the stable to take care of my cattle two hours ago, and the Lord has kept me in prayer until just now. Because of this I just know that we are going to have a revival.' Oswald Chambers continues: 'Sure enough, a revival followed just as the old man had predicted.'

Are we similarly available to God? Would we be spiritually sensitive enough to know when God is breaking in upon us to lay a burden of prayer upon our hearts for revival? Is this perhaps the real reason why revival tarries?

FURTHER STUDY

Acts 10:1–48

1. How did Cornelius make himself available to God?

2. How did Peter overcome availability problems?

Gracious and loving heavenly Father, once again You challenge the priorities in my life. Help me not to draw back, for I know that here are the issues of life and death. Help me be available, dear Lord. In Jesus' name I pray. Amen.

The spirit of prayer

FOR READING & MEDITATION – ZECHARIAH 12:1–14

'And I will pour out on the house of David and the inhabitants of Jerusalem a spirit of grace and supplication' (v10)

One of the concepts I discovered many years ago which threw a whole new light upon the subject of revival came out of the phrase found in the verse before us today: 'the spirit of grace and supplication'. The passage refers to the days of Christ's return when God will pour out His Holy Spirit upon the people of Israel so that they recognise the One they crucified as their one true Messiah. As a result of the Spirit's work in their hearts, they will be able to approach God on a level of prayer and supplication that they never before understood or experienced.

I believe something similar happens in the hearts of those who carry a great burden for revival. They are lifted out of themselves into a new dimension of praying, so that their prayers become filled with a passion and an urgency that is greater than anything they ever before knew. Sometimes this is referred to in revival literature as 'the spirit of prayer' or 'the spirit of intercession'.

Over the past few days I have asked you some deeply personal and challenging questions. Permit me to ask yet another: are you willing to let God put upon your heart a burden for revival? Would you be prepared to be enrolled in the company of those who know what it means to be involved in what we have been calling revival praying? Think long before you answer, for it could be significant in terms of time, dedication, energy, commitment and effort. Keep in mind, however, that the rewards are worth more than the cost and no one can give anything to God without experiencing something greater in return. How wonderful it would be if God used this devotional to raise up an army of intercessors seeking God's face to pour out His Spirit.

FURTHER STUDY

1 Sam 10:9–11, 19:19–24; Jude v20

1. What happened when Saul encountered the Spirit?

2. How do we pray in the Holy Spirit?

Father, help me see as I face another challenge that You not only set before me extremely high demands but You also provide the power by which I can reach them. Help me not to forget this as I reflect on Your challenge. In Jesus' name. Amen.

smallGroup central

Small groups give us an amazing opportunity to talk freely and honestly about life, the Bible and our relationship with God.

Here at CWR we believe in the great importance of these groups. We also know how we can be left scratching our heads wondering what to do with our small groups! From which topics to include, to how we can effectively explore a Bible passage in just a couple of hours - it can be a real challenge to plan, especially when life is busy.

But we want to help. So we've created **Small Group Central** - all of our small group ideas and resources in one place. You can find:

- **Free teaching:** Andy Peck, a CWR tutor, has created videos on the practicalities of leading a small group
- **Free tools:** templates, discussion starters, icebreakers - all you need to lead a group study effectively
- **Resources:** books, booklets and videos on an extensive list of themes, Bible books and life issues.

We hope it will be a one-stop shop for anyone looking for clear, easy to use, biblical inspiration for their group. Whether it's how to discuss controversial or tricky subjects or how to lead an in-depth Bible study – you can find it here at **www.smallgroupcentral.org.uk**

We would love as many people as possible to start using Small Group Central so share it with your group, leader or church today!

SAT 7 JUN

Don't wait for feelings – begin

FOR READING & MEDITATION – JEREMIAH 33:1–11

'Call to me and I will answer you and tell you great and unsearchable things you do not know.' (v3)

Following what we said yesterday about the spirit of prayer, it occurs to me that some might conclude that unless one feels strongly impelled by the Spirit to pray for revival there is no real need to do so. But as our text for today implies, whenever we see that there is a need for revival, as there was in Jeremiah's day, we are bidden to pray for it. We must be careful that we do not wait for any special moving of the Spirit to do what the Word of God plainly tells us is our spiritual duty. If a spirit of prayer is given, then fine, but we do not just wait for it to fall upon us before we begin to pray for revival.

I have come across many Christians in my time who believe that prayer is of no value unless one feels like it. They seem to think that the efficacy of prayer depends on the emotional keenness one feels as one prays. This is simply not true. D.L. Moody said: 'When it is hardest to pray, we ought to pray the hardest.' When we pray and do not really feel like it we bring to God not only our prayers but a disciplined spirit as well. We have prayed against our inclination; the self might not be pleased but God is. We must be willing to recognise feelings but not to depend on them. Feelings fluctuate with our health, the weather or the news, and our communication with heaven must not depend on something as fragile as feelings.

Having said that, I must make the point that many of those who in their prayer times begin to take up the need of revival often find themselves being gripped and seized by a depth of passion and feeling they have never known before. They begin in the natural and are caught up into the supernatural. The important thing however is to begin.

FURTHER STUDY

Dan. 6:1–28

1. What was Daniel's spiritual routine?

2. How did God respond to his faithfulness?

Father, show me even more clearly that I do not need to experience a spirit of prayer in order to pray for revival. If the spirit of prayer comes as I pray, then so be it. If it does not, I will pray anyway. Help me – in Jesus' name. Amen.

Pentecost – The God-given norm

SUN
8 JUN

FOR READING & MEDITATION – ACTS 2:5-21

'In the last days, God says, I will pour out my Spirit on all people.' (v17)

We have been seeing in our earlier devotional, that revival in part means 'wake up and live'. As you know, whenever the prefix 're' is used before a word, as in re-vival, re-animation, or re-turn, it simply means 'back again'. Revival, then, it could be said, is the Christian Church going back again to the God-given norm. And what is that 'norm'? I suggest it is nothing less than what happened on the Day of Pentecost.

Picture the scene with me as it happened on that first Whitsunday. Thousands of people fill the narrow streets of Jerusalem, drawn to the city for the celebration of the feast of Pentecost. Spiritually, however, the nation is at an all-time low. Except for Jesus and John the Baptist, no prophet has spoken in Israel for over 400 years. The disciples are gathered in an Upper Room like frightened sheep in a pen, waiting for the fulfilment of the promise Jesus had given them ten days earlier: 'You shall receive power when the Holy Spirit has come upon you' (Acts 1:8, NKJV). Suddenly the Spirit comes and transforms the timid disciples into men who are ablaze and confident.

FURTHER STUDY

Hosea 6:1-3; Acts 2:41-47

1. What was Hosea's exhortation?

2. What was the result of Pentecost?

They in turn go out into the people and witness in such a way that thousands are swept into a close and dynamic relationship with God. The very atmosphere is heavy with God's presence to such an extent that one feels anything can happen.

This was the 'norm' and this is what the Church returns to whenever a revival comes. Indeed, there is clear evidence for the fact that every revival that has taken place over the centuries since the Church has been in existence contains some feature of the Day of Pentecost.

O Father, on this, the day when Your Church celebrates the coming of the Spirit, give us we pray another Day of Pentecost. Open the windows of heaven over all nations, and pour out Your power. In Christ's name we ask it. Amen.

Christlike power

FOR READING & MEDITATION - JOHN 7:32-39

'Up to that time the Spirit had not been given, since Jesus had not yet been glorified.' (v39)

The pattern for revival is based on what God did for His people on the Day of Pentecost. But why Pentecost? Why could the pattern not be based on the many Old Testament revivals, such as those that took place under Nehemiah, Hezekiah or even David?

I believe it was because the Old Testament revivals, while arresting and reformative, did not contain enough transformative elements on which to establish a norm. The Holy Spirit – always the prime agent in any revival – relates in a limited way in Old Testament times. His ministry was special, temporary and intermittent. He came and went, providing temporary infusions of power for temporary tasks. Another aspect of the Holy Spirit's ministry in the Old Testament was the fact He came upon people from the outside as opposed to residing permanently on the inside. It was said of Samson: 'the Spirit of GOD began working in him while he was staying at a Danite camp' (Judg. 13:25 *The Message*). Yet another reason why the Spirit's ministry was limited in the Old Testament was the fact there was no perfect vehicle through whom He could reveal Himself.

FURTHER STUDY

Judg. 16:13-31; Acts 1:1-8

1. What did Samson realise?

2. What did Jesus promise?

The passage before us today draws all these strands of truth together when it says that the Spirit could not be fully given until Jesus had been glorified. Why would this be so? Because only through Jesus' life and death could God's limitless authority be properly seen and understood. Eternal authority and influence are seen not only in the context of signs, wonders and miracles, but at work on a cross, dying, suffering and overcoming sin. The power that fell at Pentecost, if it is to be the pattern for the centuries to come, must not be just power – but *Christlike* power.

O Father, thank You for sending Jesus to reveal the truth about the Holy Spirit, as well as about You, I see now so clearly that not only are You a Christlike God but the Spirit is a Christlike Spirit. I am so grateful. Amen.

Sanity as well as sanctity

FOR READING & MEDITATION – PHILIPPIANS 2:1-11

'Your attitude should be the same as that of Christ Jesus' (v5)

We saw yesterday that the Holy Spirit could not be given until Jesus had come to define the nature of the Spirit and make clear to people just what kind of Spirit He is. Jesus reveals not only the nature of the Father but also the nature of the Spirit. If God is a Christlike God, then the Spirit is also a Christlike Spirit.

Men and women, I have discovered, have some strange ideas about the Holy Spirit and the way He works in human lives. Over the years I have met some fanatical people in the Church who claimed that the Holy Spirit had been prompting them to do things which quite clearly were not appropriate. For example, I remember talking to a man some years ago who told me the Holy Spirit had instructed him to leave his wife and go and live with another woman. Clearly his understanding of the nature of the Holy Spirit needed correction and clarification.

The nature of the Spirit is determined by what we see in Jesus Christ. This is very important, for in some parts of the Church people have made the Spirit into someone who appears to be peculiar or perplexing. Why are so many Christians afraid to surrender to the Holy Spirit? They think that to do so will expose them to emotionalism or make them off-balance. But if we trust Jesus, we will recognise the Spirit as a reflection of someone we already know. So the fact that the Holy Spirit is a reflection of Jesus guarantees that when we surrender to the Spirit we are not surrendering to the unpredictable or the wild – but to balance and sanity. If we are infused by the Holy Spirit we will be made like Jesus, or it will not be the Holy Spirit but some other spirit. Jesus is not only sanctity – He is also sanity.

FURTHER STUDY

Rom. 8:1-17;
1 Pet. 1:10-12

1. How do we live in accordance with the Spirit?

2. How are the Spirit and Christ linked?

Lord Jesus, I am grateful that You have clarified the nature and character of the Holy Spirit. Help me never to forget that He is like You, and that when He comes, He comes to make me like You – balanced and sane and poised. Amen.

'In my name'

FOR READING & MEDITATION - JOHN 14:15-31

'But the Counsellor, the Holy Spirit, whom the Father will send in my name, will teach you all things' (v26)

We continue with the thought we looked at yesterday, that some people have misguided or wrong ideas about the work and nature of the Holy Spirit. I once knew a minister who had sadly become an alcoholic and could not break free. Instead of admitting the difficulty he was in and seeking help and support, he rationalised the problem and said his heavy drinking opened him up to the Holy Spirit because it lifted his inhibitions and made him more susceptible to divine revelation. I suggested that all that was happening to him was that he was getting drunk. He replied: 'Ah, some people alcohol makes drunk, but me it makes more available to God.' Unfortunately, he couldn't have been more wrong.

How thankful we are that through Christ the nature and character of the Holy Spirit has been made known. The Holy Spirit is like Jesus. As our text for today says: He is given in Christ's name. This is possibly why God could only give the Holy Spirit sparingly to men in Old Testament times; He waited until Jesus had fully revealed the nature and character of the Spirit. It is only in Jesus that we see ultimate character revealed. The Incarnation had to come before the Indwelling.

So take a good look at Jesus before you take a good look at the Holy Spirit and then you will come out with the right perspectives. There was nothing weird or strange or unbalanced about Jesus. He never over-emphasised (as do some Christians) getting guidance through visions and dreams. He got his guidance through prayer and waiting upon God. Visions and dreams may have their place in the Christian life, but only in balance.

FURTHER STUDY

Eph. 5:1-20

1. Describe the Spirit-filled life.

2. Contrast the results of imbibing wine and the Spirit.

Father, I want to thank You for clarifying for me the nature and character of the Holy Spirit. Help me not to expect You to exercise or demonstrate in my life any power that is not power Jesus would have exercised or demonstrated. Amen.

Pentecost – the only pattern

FOR READING & MEDITATION – ACTS 4:23-37

'... the place where they were meeting was shaken. And they were all filled with the Holy Spirit' (v31)

We continue exploring the issue that Pentecost, and not any of the Old Testament revelations of the Holy Spirit, is God's norm for the Church. It is important that we grasp this, because when praying for revival many Christians set their sights on happenings in the Old Testament. But while these contain interesting and helpful insights, they are not to become our pattern.

As we saw yesterday, the pattern for revival is Pentecost. The Spirit could not have been fully given in the Old Testament dispensation as this would have set a wrong pattern, and for the same reason He could not have been given in the day of Jesus' humiliation. The Spirit could only be given after the work of Jesus on earth was complete – after He had returned to the eternal throne – for that alone was the right pattern. This is why our prayers for revival and our expectations are based on Pentecost – the greatest manifestation of the Holy Spirit the world has ever known.

Do not be intimidated by those who tell you that Pentecost was a one-off experience which God does not want to repeat. As I have said, throughout the history of the Church every revival that has taken place has contained one or more of the ingredients of Pentecost. In some the dominant feature has been conviction of sin; in others, abounding joy; and in others, amazing miracles brought about through supernatural power. If God sees fit to send another revival to the world, or parts of the world, perhaps the next one will contain *all* the ingredients of Pentecost. I don't know about you, but this is something I find myself longing for with all my heart.

FURTHER STUDY

Acts 8:14-17; Acts 19:1-12

1. Why may people be ignorant of the Holy Spirit?

2. How were their experiences a pattern of Pentecost?

O Father, let my longing for another Pentecost be translated into a deeper and closer walk with You – by prayer, meditation in the Scriptures and sharing with others the concept of Your greatness and power. In Jesus' name I ask it. Amen.

Extraordinary happenings

FOR READING & MEDITATION – ACTS 2:1-4

'Suddenly a sound like the blowing of a violent wind came from heaven' (v2)

It ought to be clear by now that revival is an extraordinary work of God producing extraordinary results among a large group of people. It is vitally important that we see it in these terms, otherwise we will fall for the popular notion of calling any unusual activity of the Church by the name 'revival'.

Consider with me again the Day of Pentecost. Firstly, the extraordinary *physical manifestations* – 'a rushing mighty wind' and 'forked tongues, as of fire'. Almost every revival in history contains accounts of extraordinary physical manifestations. In the 1859 Ulster revival people would fall to the ground in the streets or the fields and would lie there motionless for hours. So astonishing were these physical phenomena that crowds gathered just to see these manifestations take place and many were converted as they witnessed God at work.

The Day of Pentecost also resulted in extraordinary preaching. One sermon preached by Peter resulted in 3,000 souls coming into the Kingdom. Sometimes, today, it takes 3,000 sermons to bring one soul into the Kingdom! In revival, leaders experience extraordinary understanding and authority pulsing through their talks. My grandfather, who was converted in the Welsh revival of 1904, told me that many of the ministers of Wales took on a new eloquence and authority during the days of revival, which quite astonished those who had previously listened to them. You may have heard some great preaching in your time, but believe me, it is nothing compared to what one hears when revival comes again. Simple statements bristle with authority; it is preaching from hearts set on fire.

FURTHER STUDY

Acts 9:1-9; 10:34-48

1. What was the experience of Paul and his companions?

2. Why was Peter astonished?

Father, whilst it is You my heart longs after, not extraordinary manifestations, I see how these things can make people in the world sit up and take notice. So for their sakes – do it again, dear Lord. Do it again. Amen.

Detained before the Eternal

FOR READING & MEDITATION – ACTS 5:1–16

'No-one else dared join them, even though they were highly regarded by the people.' (v13)

Another outcome of Pentecost was an extraordinary sense of God's holiness. Something of this is undoubtedly present in the Church at all times but when revival comes it is greatly heightened. So great was the sense of God's holiness in the early Church that, as our text for today tells us, it was felt even by those who were outside. It would be impossible, I think, to find any revival in history where an extraordinary sense of God's holiness has not been present. During the days of the revival in the United States under Charles Finney the sense of God's holiness became so overwhelming that the entire congregation of 500 rose up as one crying out, 'O God, save us – or destroy us.'

Yet another outcome of Pentecost was an extraordinary interest in prayer and in the study of the Scriptures. Prior to Pentecost, the disciples, Jews to a man, no doubt spent a good deal of time in prayer and the perusal of the Scriptures. After Pentecost, however, both prayer and the study of the Scriptures took on a new and greater importance. The Twelve agreed amongst themselves to hand over their administrative responsibilities to others in order that they might give themselves continually to prayer and the study of the Word (Acts 6:2–4).

In revival, Christians find no activity more meaningful than spending time with God in prayer and the Scriptures. Even those who gave time to prayer and daily Bible reading prior to revival find themselves gripped with a new spiritual interest and desire. As they read the Word they discover that they do not want to pull away. They are, as Moffatt translates, 'detained in the presence of the Eternal' (1 Sam. 21:7).

FURTHER STUDY

Isa. 35:8-10; Acts 17:10-12

1. What is the nature of a believer's walk?

2. What did the believers do?

Father, the more I consider the great things You are able to do, the more my heart cries out, 'Do it again, dear Lord.' But don't let my desire to see the extraordinary blind me to the joys of the ordinary. In Jesus' name I pray. Amen.

SUN
15 JUN

Dejected melancholics?

FOR READING & MEDITATION – ACTS 8:1-8

'So there was great joy in that city.' (v8)

Yet another outcome of Pentecost was extraordinary energy and enthusiasm. One has only to read the pages of the Acts of the Apostles to feel the pulse and joy that characterised the early disciples. It surfaces in many places, one of which is the text before us today.

The early Church was excited about everything that was connected with God and His Kingdom. They were excited about Jesus, about the coming of His Spirit, about the establishment of His Kingdom, and about the promise of His coming again. They were gripped by an intense earnestness and a spirit of expectation. The God who had raised up Jesus from the dead had raised them also from their own graves of sin. The authority that had elevated Christ to the heavens and placed Him at the right hand of the Father was working in them with all its invigorating empowerment.

This is also the way it is in times of revival. As God pours Himself out, people repent of their sins and find peace with God, it invariably happens that there is extraordinary happiness and joy. Let no one think that revival is associated with heaviness and gloom. There may be a period of mourning for sin but this is soon followed by waves of contentment and peace. It is surely amongst the most tragic misrepresentations of truth that historians should write that in times of revival Christians act like dejected melancholics. The truth is that in revival, Christians, like their brothers and sisters in the first century, have to defend themselves against the charge of being drunk. Very few of us come under that dark suspicion nowadays, but it is hardly to our credit that there is rarely any need to stress the distinction.

FURTHER STUDY

Acts 13:42-52; Rom. 14:17-18

1. How is the Holy Spirit linked to joy?

2. What is the nature of God's Kingdom?

O Father, as far as it is possible outside of the great wave of revival, let me be filled with the same spirit of energy and excitement that pervaded the early Church. For Your own dear name's sake I ask it. Amen.

How do revivals happen?

MON
16 JUN

FOR READING & MEDITATION – PSALM 85:1–13

'Will you not revive us again, that your people may rejoice in you?' (v6)

Before moving on in our devotions on revival we pause for a moment to remind ourselves of some of the issues we have been considering. Revival, we have said, is like God bending down to the dying embers of a fire about to go out and breathing into it until it bursts again into flame. The blueprint for revival is Pentecost, which was an extraordinary visitation of God accompanied by extraordinary happenings and manifestations. God is after the recovery of New Testament Christianity and He has invariably used revivals to this end. One reason why revival is important is because the Church turns from its first love and falls into decline. And when revival comes it achieves, sometimes in a few weeks, what could never have been achieved in years of human or ordinary Christian activity.

The next question to consider is this: how does a revival happen? Is it something that forms in the minds of devoted Christian people and is then brought into being by powerful intercessory prayer? Or is it something that originates in the mind of God and comes down to earth irrespective of the desires or the prayer life of His people?

I have no hesitation in saying that in my opinion revival begins in the mind of God. It is something that God plans and purposes; men and women have little to do with it. There are many things that Christians, by dedicated and committed spiritual effort, can bring to pass in the Church, but revival is not one of them. Such things as evangelism, preaching, teaching, and counselling, are work that we do for God; revival is work that God does for us.

FURTHER STUDY

John 3:1–8; Rev. 2:1–7

1. Why can we not tell when or where revival happens?

2. What was good and bad about the Ephesian church?

Father, let the wonder of Your sovereignty and power sink deep into my soul today. Help me see how much bigger and greater You are than my imagination could ever conceive. In Christ's name I pray. Amen.

The place of prayer

FOR READING & MEDITATION – ZECHARIAH 10:1-8

'Ask the LORD for rain in the springtime' (v1)

We continue looking at the question: how do revivals happen? A revival is a sovereign act of God in the sense that it is initiated by Him and not by the Church. It is at this point – the sovereignty of God – that Christians tend to differ in their thinking about revival. One school of thought says: 'Revival is a sovereign act of God and there is absolutely nothing that man has to do with it. God sends revival when He wills and does not consult or confer with any of His creation.' Many of the great Welsh revivalists like Christmas Evans, Daniel Rowlands, John Elias, Thomas Charles Edwards, and John Evans subscribed to this view.

Another school of thought says: 'Revival can happen any time the Church wants it – providing she is willing to pay the price.' The great revivalist Charles Finney believed this. 'The Church,' he said, 'can have a revival whenever it wills, for revival is like a crop of wheat – the farmer sows and then in due course the wheat comes up. When we are willing to sow the seeds of prayer and travail in the red furrows of God's fields then as sure as night follows day – we will have a revival.'

The truth, so I believe, lies somewhere between these two opposing views. Revival is a sovereign act of God in the sense that He alone originates it, but I also believe myself that God deigns to hand over to His people the responsibility of bringing it down from heaven to earth on the wings of faith-filled, inspired prayer. Every great outpouring of the Holy Spirit – Pentecost included – began in the mind of God but broke through on earth at the point of passionate and persevering prayer.

FURTHER STUDY

Gal. 6:7-10; Col. 1:28-29

1. How might revival be linked to sowing and reaping?

2. How may we combine God's power with human effort?

Father, if so much depends upon prayer, then wake me up to its power and its importance. Help me this day to catch a new vision of what it means to be an intercessor. In Christ's name I ask it. Amen.

NEXT ISSUE

EVERY DAY WITH JESUS
Jul/Aug 2014

Poet of Hope

Like us, Jeremiah lived in difficult times, yet he remained true to God. Do we, like Jeremiah, have the certainty that God has chosen us for His tasks?

In this issue, Selwyn reflects on the life of Jeremiah and his challenges of facing the independence and complacency of the people of Judah. Jeremiah was lonely, threatened and attacked as he spoke out. Learn more about prayer, obedience and his security in God – security which can be ours, too.

Also available as eBook/ eSubscription

OBTAIN YOUR COPY FROM
CWR, a Christian bookshop or National Distributor.
If you would like to take out a subscription, see the order form at the back of these notes.

Involved in government

FOR READING & MEDITATION – EPHESIANS 3:1-13

'... that now, through the church, the manifold wisdom of God should be made known' (v10)

Today we ask ourselves: what does it mean when we say that God is sovereign? Sovereignty simply means to possess supreme power. What we have to be careful about when we talk of the sovereignty of God is that we do not fall for the idea (as some have) that this is God's *greatest* attribute; His greatest attribute is love. And because He is love this means (so I believe) not only that it dictates and defines all His characteristics and His actions but that He delights to have His redeemed children become involved with Him, even in a comparatively small way, in the bringing to pass of His purposes.

Anyone who writes on the subject of revival has to come to a point where these two great and important truths – the sovereignty of God and the involvement of man – have to be brought together. I am at that point right now. A way of thinking about this issue which has always satisfied me is to see these two thoughts like two rails that run from one end of the Scriptures to the other. One rail is the sovereignty of God and the other, the involvement of man. If you try to keep to only one rail you finish up being derailed. Those who focus only on the sovereignty of God inevitably result in minimising the responsibility of man. And those who focus only on the involvement of man end up minimising the sovereignty of God.

When we move along the rails, making sure that we do not place a disproportionate emphasis on either truth, then we are more likely to arrive at sounder judgments and correct conclusions. God is sovereign but He is also a loving sovereign and by virtue of this fact delights to involve His people in the affairs of government.

FURTHER STUDY

Mark 16:15-20; 2 Cor. 4:1-7

1. What was the experience of the disciples?

2. What did Paul explain?

Gracious and loving Father, how can we Your Church sufficiently thank You for the fact that You love us enough to involve us in Your government? Help us see that we are there not because we deserve, but because You desire it. Amen.

'Nothing ... except through prayer'

THURS **19 JUN**

FOR READING & MEDITATION – COLOSSIANS 4:2-15

'Devote yourselves to prayer' (v2)

A single sentence written by the great John Wesley, which I have quoted on numerous occasions, has helped me more than anything else to balance the two great truths we referred to yesterday – the sovereignty of God and the responsibility of man. Here is the statement which Wesley made: 'God does nothing redemptively in the world except through prayer.'

Permit me to put into my own words what I think he was saying: whenever God wants to bring His purposes to pass here on earth He does not act arbitrarily, but touches the hearts of praying people and then ushers in His purposes across the bridge of prayer. God may be sovereign but He is not dictatorial or capricious. He can no more act against His nature and the principles He has established in the world than He could make a square circle or an aged infant. There are some things impossible even for God, and acting independently of the principle of prayer is one of them. This is why prayer and revival are so inseparably linked. I know of no revival that is not connected in some way with God-inspired, believing, intercessory prayer, full of the vibrant characteristics that we explored earlier in this issue.

This, then, is how I see God's sovereignty and man's responsibility being brought together in harmony: when God decides that in the interests of His people a spiritual revival is necessary, He lays a burden of prayer upon the hearts of His children – it may only be comparatively few – so that their prayers become the bridge across which revival flows. Let Wesley's famous statement ring in your heart once again: 'God does nothing redemptively in the world – except through prayer.'

FURTHER STUDY

Exod. 2:23-3:7; Ezra 8:21-23

1. What preceded God's deliverance of His people?

2. What was Ezra's experience?

God, I see that Your purposes are not arbitrary or capricious but the very expression of Your nature. Amid the splendour of Your majesty and sovereignty I feel a heartbeat – a heartbeat of love. Thank You, dear Father. Amen.

The wider context of revival

FOR READING & MEDITATION – 2 CHRONICLES 7:12–22

'if my people ... will humble themselves and pray ... then will I hear from heaven and will forgive their sin' (v14)

We continue meditating on the question: if revival is a sovereign act of God (and I believe it is), does this mean that the people of God have no part whatsoever to play in it? My answer to that question is a categorical 'No'. Revival is a sovereign act of God in the sense that He allows it in His time, where and when and upon whom He wills, but a study of revivals in the past, both in Scripture and in the history of the Church, shows that revival often follows the prevailing prayers of God's people – those revival or extraordinary prayers which we have already explored.

The central condition of the verse before us today is, 'if my people ... *pray*'. When Evan Roberts was asked the secret of revival he said: 'There is no secret: ask and you shall receive.' Matthew Henry, the renowned Bible commentator, wrote a good deal about this particular point and summed it up in what I consider to be a powerful and memorable statement: 'When God intends a great mercy for His people, the first thing He does is set them a-praying.' God is the only one who can initiate revival, but the inspired intercession of His people is the ramp over which it flows into the Church.

FURTHER STUDY

Neh. 1:1–2:9

1. What caused Nehemiah to pray?

2. Contrast his two prayers.

It is recognised that sovereignty is not the only thing at work in revival – love is also at work. We are dealing with a God who is big-hearted and generous in doing good, as well as omnipotent – never forget that! Once we see revival in this wider context – the context of love – we begin to understand why it is that God inspires strong intercessory prayer in the hearts of His people prior to revival. He just loves for His children to be involved with Him in the bringing about of His purposes.

O Father, I am grateful that You are a God who not only hears our prayers but delights to respond to them. Cause our prayers to be Spirit-inspired that we may build with You a cooperative commonwealth. In Jesus' name I ask it. Amen.

The burden of revival

SAT
21 JUN

FOR READING & MEDITATION – JEREMIAH 23:33-40

'But you must not mention "the oracle of the LORD" again, because every man's word becomes his oracle' (v36)

We ended yesterday by saying that God inspires strong intercessory prayer in the hearts of His people prior to revival because He loves His children to be involved with Him in the bringing about of His purposes, and that it is not in God's nature to ignore the great principle of prayer which He Himself has established in the universe. At the risk of being tedious, let me make the point again: although revival begins in the sovereign purposes of God, it comes into the world through the doorway of inspired prayer.

John Wallace, Principal of the Bible College I attended prior to entering the ministry, used to say: 'Before somebody can experience a blessing, somebody has to bear a burden.' He used to illustrate the point in this way: 'Before deliverance came to the nation of Israel when they were in Egypt, Moses had to bear a burden. Before the great temple of God could be built in Jerusalem, Solomon was called to bear a burden. Before the sins of the world could be removed, Christ had to bear a burden. *Before somebody can experience a blessing, somebody has to bear a burden.*'

This is a principle that can be traced throughout the whole narrative of the Bible – from Genesis to Revelation burdens precede blessing. It can be seen at work, too, in the history of all religious revivals. Before God comes from heaven to work in extraordinary ways He places the burden of revival on the hearts of His people. And who does He choose to carry this burden? You can be sure that they will be men and women who are drawn to prayer and understand something of its power and potential. Would you, I wonder, be one?

FURTHER STUDY

Luke 2:25-35; Gal. 2:1-10

1. What burden did Simeon bear?

2. Compare and contrast the burdens of Peter and Paul.

Gracious Father, You know how my heart shrinks from such a great challenge as this. All I can say is – I am willing to be made willing. Help me, dear Father. In Jesus' name. Amen.

SUN 22 JUN

God works through authority

FOR READING & MEDITATION – EPHESIANS 1:3-10

'… who has blessed us in the heavenly realms with every spiritual blessing in Christ.' (v3)

Another reason why God takes care to involve His people when He initiates a revival is because He is deeply committed to working in and through His Church – not behind her back. I said a few weeks ago, you might remember, that our view of the Church will greatly influence our view of revival and now I must make the point again.

The Church (so I believe) is God's agent in the world through which His plans and purposes are to be demonstrated and expressed. She is here to model to the world what the Kingdom of God is all about. God is committed to working through her and not around her and no matter how lethargic His people become, He will not withdraw from that commitment. If God wanted to exercise His sovereignty (and nothing else) then He could burst in upon His Church in times of declension without regard to anyone. But, as we have seen, there are other characteristics in God beside sovereignty – love and respect being just two.

If there is one thing more than anything else that impresses me about God's dealings with men in the Bible it is the fact that He greatly respects the authority He establishes, even though that authority does not act in the way He desires. It would have been easy for Him to have swept aside the Old Testament kings and priests of ancient Israel who had failed to do His bidding, but patiently and lovingly He worked to involve them in His purposes. If God did that with His earthly people, Israel, then I cannot conceive of Him doing any less with His heavenly people, the Church. He will make sure the Church is represented and involved in every single spiritual project that goes on in the universe.

FURTHER STUDY

Eph. 1:11-23, 3:1-13

1. What is the authority of the Church?

2. How does God administer His grace?

Gracious Father, Your commitment never to go behind the back of Your Church to accomplish Your purposes staggers and amazes me. My heart says: a God who works like this can have all there is of me to have. My heart is Yours. Amen.

The magnetism of heaven

MON
23 JUN

FOR READING & MEDITATION – ACTS 2:36–47

'... they were cut to the heart and said to Peter and the other apostles, "Brothers, what shall we do?"' (v37)

An important and final question which we must look at before we close our meditations on the theme of revival is this: how great is our need at this moment in history for a great spiritual awakening? I would say that in the UK and most countries of the world it is very great. If revival is an extraordinary movement of the Holy Spirit bestowed upon the Church by a sovereign God, then when is God most likely to demonstrate this extraordinary work? Is it not at a time of extraordinary need? Such a time, I suggest, is upon us now. If I understand contemporary Christianity at all, then it is my conviction that the need for revival is not only great but urgent and desperate.

Take, for example, the issue of evangelism. It should be a matter of the deepest concern that with all its evangelistic efforts (even Alpha with its world-wide reach) the Church is only touching a small proportion of the community. The fact that in some countries many are being converted should not obscure the fact that great masses of people remain unreached. We expend great effort and spend large sums of money on evangelistic outreach and programmes, all of which is right, but the results are rarely what deep down in our hearts we long for. We are thankful, of course, for those who are being won to Christ but it concerns us that in proportion to the population the results are but a drop in a bucket.

Revival would change all that. Although revival, as we saw, is different from evangelism, you can be sure that when revival comes the unconverted will crowd into the churches, drawn not by human persuasion but by the magnetism of heaven.

FURTHER STUDY

Acts 2:1–6, 5:12–26

1. What happened at the first Pentecost?

2. How did ordinary people respond to the first disciples?

O Father, give us another Pentecost so that as in Bible days preachers will not call on sinners, but sinners call on the preachers asking, 'What must I do to be saved?' In Christ's name we ask it. Amen.

TUES
24 JUN

A time of spiritual tragedy

FOR READING & MEDITATION – LUKE 6:12-19

'... Jesus went out to a mountainside to pray, and spent the night praying to God.' (v12)

Another issue in today's Church which makes the need for revival urgent and desperate is the way in which the Church, generally speaking, has become more activity (and possibly more social action) oriented than prayer oriented. There can be little doubt that today's Church has learned a good deal about how to organise events, how to get the best results from advertising, how to research and target specific objectives, how to identify trends and make predictions based on those trends ... and so on. What has not been quite so good is teaching people how to pray – to pray powerfully and effectively for God to make His mighty power and presence known in the world. I must point out again that I am speaking generally, for I know there will be many reading these lines who come from churches which are exceptions to what I am saying.

Now do not hear me speaking in condemning tones of today's Church in the areas I have mentioned. It is good to research and study underlying principles, such as, for example, what makes for effective evangelism or how churches grow. There can be little doubt that the study of these things has greatly contributed to the life and development of the Church in this generation.

Here, however, is the problem – it is so easy for us to become satisfied by our successes in the field of study and research that our satisfaction can deaden our desire and rob us of a sense of need to see God work in a sovereign and extraordinary way through revival. We are in a time of spiritual tragedy when our activity becomes a blockage to His activity. Only prayer can keep our eyes fully on Him.

FURTHER STUDY

Psa. 20:1-9; Luke 5:13-16

1. What do we rely on?

2. What was Jesus' regular practice?

Father, forgive us that we so easily let our successes move our focus away from what You can do. Bring us to our knees – metaphorically and literally. In Jesus' name we pray. Amen.

When *we* become god

FOR READING & MEDITATION – PROVERBS 16:17–25

'Pride goes before destruction, a haughty spirit before a fall.' (v18)

Another issue in today's Church which makes the need for revival urgent and desperate is an unconscious self-dependency. I say *unconscious* because most Christians do not know that they are doing it – but they are, nevertheless.

Here is how it develops: we learn or discover ways of doing things for God that make us feel good. At first, the most important thing is not the feelings we get but the significance of the task in which we are engaged. Gradually, however, we become preoccupied with the positive feelings that our actions give us and the significance of what we are doing takes second place. Subtly the tables have been turned – we move from depending on God for our significance to the good feelings we get from what we are doing. Can you see the danger in this? And whatever we depend upon to hold our lives together and make them work – that is our god. So it can be said that when self-dependency rules our hearts then we become god. If I were asked to name the biggest single problem in the Church today I would unhesitatingly point to this – the tendency to depend on self rather than God to make our lives work.

Revival would change all this. In times of great spiritual awakening unconscious motives are brought into consciousness and men and women see themselves as they really are. The proud become humble, the arrogant become unassuming, and the self-dependent become God-dependent. One of the most difficult tasks of a Christian counsellor is to help people realise what they are hiding behind and come out from behind it to become their real, authentic selves. It sometimes takes months, even years, to get that point across. In revival God does it in one fell swoop.

FURTHER STUDY

Judg. 7:1–8; Isa. 50:7–11

1. Why did God reduce Gideon's army?

2. Why do we prefer our light to God's darkness?

Gracious and loving heavenly Father, I don't want to wait for a revival in order that I might become a more real and aware person. You have my permission to do it this hour. Give me my own personal revival – today. In Jesus' name. Amen.

The battle for the Bible

FOR READING & MEDITATION – PSALM 119:89–96

'Your word, O LORD, is eternal; it stands firm in the heavens.' (v89)

Yet another issue in today's Church which makes the need for revival urgent and desperate is a growing loss of confidence in the Scriptures. Surveys reveal that people, including Christians, are reading their Bibles less. Of course, not all churches have moved away from the authority of the Scriptures, but we must face the fact that many have and are.

'We are slowly reaching the position,' says one writer, 'where the Christian who is orthodox in his beliefs and convictions, who holds the Bible in the central tradition of the Christian faith is considered to be a dogmatic reactionary, a stubborn anti-intellectualist, an obscurantist to be pitied and derided. The gospel which brings men to a personal knowledge of Christ and to the joyful experience of the new birth has to be fought for in the very inner councils of the historic denominations. In conditions such as these it would be a glib and shallow mind that dared to say a revival is not our greatest need.'

Revival brings with it a new confidence and a new faith and hunger for the truths found in Scriptures. People who are moved by the Holy Spirit in times of great spiritual awakening invariably find their faith and understanding of the Bible being greatly quickened. An Irishman who was involved in Ireland in the mid 1800s said: 'I used to read the Bible before revival came, but after I came in touch with the Holy Spirit the Bible became a new and different book. It was as if God had taken it up to heaven, rewritten it and handed it back to me. I now know it is inspired because it inspires me.' That is not the only reason, of course, why we know it is inspired but it is impressive nevertheless.

FURTHER STUDY

John 20:30–31; 2 Tim. 3:14–17; 2 Pet. 1:20–21

1. What is the purpose of Scripture?

2. What is the origin of Scripture?

Father, it is difficult to see how the battle for the Bible can be won apart from an outpouring of Your Holy Spirit. Your people need to be revived, refreshed and enlightened. Let it happen, dear Lord – soon. In Jesus' name. Amen.

The sound of marching

FOR READING & MEDITATION – 2 SAMUEL 5:17–25

'... when you hear the sound of marching in the tops of the mulberry trees, then you shall advance quickly' (v24 NKJV)

We have seen how urgent and desperate is the need for revival, and this leads to the inevitable question: will we see another great spiritual awakening in our own day and generation? I cannot say with certainty, but I most definitely would like to see it. There are signs that a revival is on the way, but before looking at them, pause with me to focus on the passage that is before us today.

Soon after David had been made king over Israel he was threatened by the Philistines. His first concern was to find what God wanted him to do about it, and after asking God for instructions and getting divine permission to proceed, he led a bold frontal attack that carried the day. Later, however, the Philistines returned and took up the position that they had occupied before. Without presuming on past guidance, David again sought God's direction and obtained permission to attack. However, this time he was led to make a detour and take up a position behind the enemy, near the mulberry (or balsam) trees. God said: 'When you hear the sound of marching in the tops of the mulberry trees, then bestir yourselves, for then has the Lord gone out before you to smite the army of the Philistines' (v24 Amplified).

These two battles illustrate the difference between the every day life activity of the Holy Spirit in the Church and the way He operates in revival. In the first we see David acting under God's direction and with His enabling. In the second it is God who takes the field and David follows on behind gathering up the spoils of victory. We have witnessed for decades the every day life operation of the Holy Spirit in the Church; the time has now come when we prepare for revival.

FURTHER STUDY

Acts 2:42–47

1. What did the disciples do?

2. What did God do?

Father, quicken my faith to believe for an outpouring of the Spirit as great if not greater than at Pentecost. I want to live in Your Word and Your Word to live in me. Fill Your Church with Your glory – and let it overflow. Amen.

SAT 28 JUN

Three signs of coming revival

FOR READING & MEDITATION – PSALM 102:1–17

'You will ... have compassion on Zion ... her stones are dear to your servants; her very dust moves them to pity' (v13–14)

We saw yesterday that before God came down and intervened in the battle against the Philistines He gave David a sign that He was about to move in a supernatural way against the enemy. The sign was a 'sound of marching in the tops of the mulberry trees'. I am emboldened to say that I believe God is giving us at this hour in history some clear sign from heaven that He is about to move in great power throughout the world.

The first sign I see is a deep and accelerating interest among the people of God in the subject of revival. Almost every Christian leader I have spoken to recently has talked to me about his or her concern for a spiritual revival. I hear it also in the new worship songs that are being written for the Church. God is touching the hearts of His people in a fresh and wonderful way to pray and expect a great Holy Spirit revival.

The second sign I see is a deep desire amongst Christians to forget denominational differences and identify themselves simply as brothers and sisters in Christ. The preparation of the first disciples at Pentecost came as they were all 'with one accord' in one place (Acts 2:1, AV), and this is how I believe it is going to be in the next great outpouring.

A third sign I see is a growing desire in the hearts of believers everywhere to pray and intercede for revival. It is one thing to be interested in revival; it is another to be interested enough to give time to pray and intercede for it. When God finds those who are as concerned for revival as God's people were about the stones and dust of Zion (as our passage for today points out) it will not be long before those who mourn will be comforted – by divine intervention.

FURTHER STUDY

2 Kings 22:1–8, 23:1–3; Psa. 84:1–12

1. How did Josiah lead a revival?

2. What was the Psalmist's concern?

My Father and my God, deepen my conviction that revival is not just a dream but a reality. You have done it before and You can do it again. I believe – help Thou my unbelief. In Christ's name I ask it. Amen.

The watchman on the walls

SUN **29 JUN**

FOR READING & MEDITATION – ISAIAH 42:1–9

'See ... new things I declare; before they spring into being I announce them to you.' (v9)

'There is a vital faith element which is always in evidence in the days preceding a revival,' says Arthur Wallis in his book *Rain from Heaven*, and the stimulus for that faith is provided by those whom we may call the watchmen on the walls.

In Bible times the watchmen were the ones who stood on the walls of Jerusalem during the night so that they could report any signs of enemy activity and if necessary alert the rest of the inhabitants of the city. The watchmen were also the first ones to see the grey streaks of dawn and in its light were able to assess the current situation in a way that those in the city could not.

Just as Jerusalem had its watchmen, so too does the modern-day Church. They are the seers, the prophets, the intercessors, who are constantly on watch and report to us their findings. I have never regarded myself as one of this favoured group, but I have known many who are. They tell me that like Elijah of old they see 'a cloud the size of a man's hand' scudding across the heavens and know that soon, perhaps sooner than we think, we shall see a deluge such as we have never seen before. I believe them, for my own spirit witnesses to what they say.

Charles Finney tells the story of a woman in New Jersey who felt that God was about to send revival to her town. She encouraged the leaders to arrange some special meetings and when they refused she went ahead herself, getting a carpenter to make seats so that she could have meetings in her house. He had hardly finished before the Spirit of God fell upon the community with great power. How could this woman have been so sure? She was a watchman – a watchman of God.

FURTHER STUDY

2 Chron. 29:1–11, 27–36

1. How did Hezekiah lead a revival?

2. What was a particular cause of rejoicing?

Father, I may not be in the category of a watchman but help me keep so close to You that I will be able to hear Your faintest whisper. This I ask in Christ's peerless and precious name. Amen.

Keep your eyes on the tide

FOR READING & MEDITATION – PSALM 110:1-7

'Your troops will be willing on your day of battle' (v3)

On this our final day together we return to the question we posed on the first day of our meditations: has God something bigger for us than we are at present seeing? I hope I have convinced you that He has! How can we be open to receiving it? It comes at the precise moment God appoints but it is carried down from heaven on the wings of God-inspired prayer. Dr A.T. Pierson said, 'From the Day of Pentecost until now, there has not been one great spiritual awakening in any land which has not begun in a union of prayer though only among two or three, and no such outward or upward movement has continued after such prayer meetings have declined.' Revivals are born in prayer and sustained by prayer.

Just as there are signs given by Jesus which point us toward His second coming, so there are signs that tell us He is not far from reviving His whole Church. In the early days of the Salvation Army in France, the eldest daughter of General Booth, known by her French rank as the Maréchale, found herself at one point in an extremely discouraging situation. She wrote to General Booth asking for his advice, which came in these words: 'Take your eyes off the waves and fix them on the tide.'

My brothers and sisters, I give you now the same advice. Don't let your eyes become focused on the waves, with their rise and fall or their advances or retreats. Keep your eyes on the tide and ask yourself: is it rising? I think if you look with the eye of faith you will see that it is. When it breaks I pray that it will not find you or me unprepared, but that we shall be a people who are willing in the day of God's power.

FURTHER STUDY

Ezek. 36:22-38; Hos. 10:12

1. How can ruins come to life?

2. What time is it?

Father, what can I say? I don't know whether I will live to see a worldwide revival but I want to live to experience a personal revival. Take me on to know You in a greater way than I have ever known You before. In Christ's name. Amen.

ORDER FORM

EDWJ M/J 2014

4 EASY WAYS TO ORDER:

1. Phone in your credit card order: **01252 784710** (Mon-Fri, 9.30am - 5pm)
2. Visit our Online Store at **www.cwr.org.uk/store**
3. Send this form together with your payment to:
   CWR, Waverley Abbey House, Waverley Lane, Farnham, Surrey GU9 8EP
4. Visit your local Christian bookshop

or a list of our National Distributors, who supply countries outside the UK, visit www.cwr.org.uk/distributors

YOUR DETAILS (REQUIRED FOR ORDERS AND DONATIONS)

Full name: **CWR ID No.** (if known):

Home Address:

Postcode:

Telephone No. (for queries): **Email:**

PUBLICATIONS

TITLE	QTY	PRICE	TOTAL
		Total publications	

All CWR adult Bible-reading notes are also available in ebook and email subscription format. Visit www.cwr.org.uk for further information.

UK p&p: up to £24.99 = **£2.99**; £25.00 and over = **FREE**

Elsewhere p&p: up to £10 = **£4.95**; £10.01 - £50 = **£6.95**; £50.01 - £99.99 = **£10**; £100 and over = **£30**

Please allow 14 days for delivery

Total publications and p&p A

SUBSCRIPTIONS* (NON DIRECT DEBIT)

	QTY	PRICE (INCLUDING P&P)			TOTAL
		UK	**Europe**	**Elsewhere**	
Every Day with Jesus (1yr, 6 issues)		£15.95	£19.95	Please contact nearest National Distributor or CWR direct	
Large Print *Every Day with Jesus* (1yr, 6 issues)		£15.95	£19.95		
Inspiring Women Every Day (1yr, 6 issues)		£15.95	£19.95		
Life Every Day (Jeff Lucas) (1yr, 6 issues)		£15.95	£19.95		
Cover to Cover Every Day (1yr, 6 issues)		£15.95	£19.95		
Mettle: 14-18s (1yr, 3 issues)		£14.50	£16.60		
YP's: 11-15s (1yr, 6 issues)		£15.95	£19.95		
Topz: 7-11s (1yr, 6 issues)		£15.95	£19.95		

Total Subscriptions (Subscription prices already include postage and packing) **B**

Please circle which bimonthly issue you would like your subscription to commence from:
Jan/Feb Mar/Apr May/Jun Jul/Aug Sep/Oct Nov/Dec

*Only use this section for subscriptions paid for by credit/debit card or cheque. For Direct Debit subscriptions see overleaf.

CONTINUED OVERLEAF >>

<< SEE PREVIOUS PAGE FOR START OF ORDER FORM

PAYMENT DETAILS

☐ I enclose a cheque/PO made payable to CWR for the amount of: **£** ______

☐ Please charge my credit/debit card.

Cardholder's name (in BLOCK CAPITALS) ______

Card No. ______

Expires end ______ Security Code ______

GIFT TO CWR

☐ Please send me an acknowledgement of my gift **C** ______

GIFT AID (YOUR HOME ADDRESS REQUIRED, SEE OVERLEAF)

giftaid it

I am a UK taxpayer and want CWR to reclaim the tax on all my donations for the four years prior to this year **and on** all donations I make from the date of this Gift Aid declaration until further notice.*

Taxpayer's Full Name (in BLOCK CAPITALS) ______

Signature ______ **Date** ______

*I understand I must pay an amount of Income/Capital Gains Tax at least equal to the tax the charity reclaims in the tax year.

GRAND TOTAL (Total of A, B, & C) ______

SUBSCRIPTIONS BY DIRECT DEBIT (UK BANK ACCOUNT HOLDERS ONLY)

Subscriptions cost £15.95 (except *Mettle*: £14.50) for one year for delivery within the UK. Please tick relevant boxes and fill in the form

☐ *Every Day with Jesus* (1yr, 6 issues)
☐ Large Print *Every Day with Jesus* (1yr, 6 issues)
☐ *Inspiring Women Every Day* (1yr, 6 issues)
☐ *Life Every Day* (Jeff Lucas) (1yr, 6 issues)
☐ *Cover to Cover Every Day* (1yr, 6 issues)
☐ *Mettle*: 14-18s (1yr, 3 issues)
☐ *YP's*: 11-15s (1yr, 6 issues)
☐ *Topz*: 7-11s (1yr, 6 issues)

Issue to commence

☐ Jan/Feb ☐ Jul/Aug
☐ Mar/Apr ☐ Sep/Oct
☐ May/Jun ☐ Nov/De

CWR

Instruction to your Bank or Building Society to pay by Direct Debit

DIREC Debi

Please fill in the form and send to: CWR, Waverley Abbey House, Waverley Lane, Farnham, Surrey GU9 8EP

Name and full postal address of your Bank or Building Society

To: The Manager Bank/Building Society

Address

Postcode

Name(s) of Account Holder(s)

Branch Sort Code

Bank/Building Society account number

Originator's Identification Number

4 2 0 4 8 7

Reference

Instruction to your Bank or Building Society

Please pay CWR Direct Debits from the account detailed in this Instruction to the safeguards assured by the Direct Debit Guarantee.

I understand that this Instruction may remain with CWR and, if so, details wi passed electronically to my Bank/Building Society.

Signature(s)

Date

Banks and Building Societies may not accept Direct Debit Instructions for some types of account